4 Sequential Spelling

serve
reserve
preserve
conserve
deserve
service

By Don McCabe

Teacher's Guide
Revised Edition

Copyright ©2011 *Wave 3 Learning*, Inc.
Copyright ©2008, 2003, 1995, 1975 AVKO Educational Research Foundation, Inc.
Printed in the United States of America.

Permission is hereby given for individual parents, teachers, tutors, and educators to reproduce any list for home or classroom use only. Reproduction of these lists for entire schools or school districts is strictly forbidden.

1 Printing   Year 11

Publisher's Cataloging in Publication Data

McCabe, Donald J., *Sequential Spelling*.—Rev. ed., Arlington Heights, IL:
Wave 3 Learning, Inc. c2011.
      Volume 1 of a 7 Volume series.

1. Spelling—Miscellanea. 2. Reading—Miscellanea. 3. Curriculum—Miscellanea 4. Literacy and Tutor Reference Tool.
Library of Congress Subject Headings: Spelling, Curriculum
Library of Congress Classification Number: LB1050.2F79
Library of Congress Card Number: To be determined
Dewey Decimal Classification Number 428.4
ISBN: 9781935943129

About *Sequential Spelling*

Sequential Spelling is a research-based system rooted in the classic Orton-Gillingham approach to learning. Developed by Don McCabe, former Executive Director of the AVKO Educational Research Foundation, the curriculum provides multi-sensory spelling instruction. The student learns sets of words that share patterns of spelling rather than thematically related lists of words. This methodology enables the student with a learning difference to focus on learning a given sequence of letters, how they sound, and the words they appear in.

About this Edition

This edition of the *Sequential Spelling* series has been expanded. Each level now has a coordinating student workbook, complete with a daily "Using Your Words" activity. The teaching methodology described in the earlier edition has remained the same; however, the teacher guide now includes an answer key. We have also replaced some of the words used in the original edition with other words from *The Patterns of English Spelling* (a related product available from *Wave 3 Learning*).

Marjorie Lock, Editor
Wave 3 Learning
January 2011

Table of Contents

To the Teacher 5

    Overview 5

    Hallmarks of *Sequential Spelling* 5

Teaching the Lessons 6

    Materials Needed 6

    Lesson Time 6

    Lesson Preparation 6

    Lesson Format 6

    Progress Evaluation 7

    About the Teacher Text 7

Customizing *Sequential Spelling* for Your Student 8

Spelling Lists 9

Answer Key 59

Frequently Used Spelling Rules 72

To the Teacher

OVERVIEW

Sequential Spelling uses word families or word patterns as its teaching method. The student learns the phonics sounds necessary for decoding words while learning to spell. For example, if you can teach the word **at** you can also teach:

bat	bats	batted	batting		
cat	cats				
scat	scats				
flat	flats	flatted	flatting		
pat	pats	patted	patting		
spat	spats				
mat	mats	matted	matting		
rat	rats	ratted	ratting		
batter	batters	battered	battering	battery	batteries
flatter	flatters	flattered	flattering	flattery	
matter	matters	mattered	mattering		
battle	battles	battled	battling		
cattle					
rattle	rattles	rattled	rattling		

similarly, from the word **act** you can build:

act	acts	acted	acting	active	action
fact	facts				
tract	tracts	traction			
attract	attracts	attracted	attracting	attractive	attraction
distract	distracts	distracted	distracting	distraction	
extract	extracts	extracted	extracting	extractive	extraction
subtract	subtracts	subtracted	subtracting	subtraction	
contract	contracts	contracted	contracting	contraction	

Spelling rules are not specifically taught in this curriculum. Rather, they are learned as part of the daily spelling lesson. A description of some of the more frequently used spelling rules is included at the end of this Guide.

HALLMARKS OF *SEQUENTIAL SPELLING*

- daily spelling tests with immediate feedback
- multi-sensory teaching (audio, visual, kinesthetic and oral) of spelling patterns
- base words are introduced first, then the endings for them (-s, -ed, -ing) on subsequent days.
- 180 lessons per level
- levels are not matched to grade level. Most students should begin at level 1.

Teaching the Lessons

MATERIALS NEEDED:

- Easel or dry erase board
- Different colored markers
- Student Workbook or notebook paper
- Teacher's guide

LESSON TIME:

15-20 minutes

LESSON PREPARATION:

Review the words for the spelling test before beginning the lesson to familiarize yourself with tricky spellings, homophones, etc.

Have students open their workbooks and find the page for the day's lesson. If they are using notebook paper for the spelling test, use one sheet per lesson.

LESSON FORMAT:

Each day will consist of a spelling test, building to twenty-five words by lesson 9. Rather than teaching the spelling of each word, teachers should concentrate on teaching the basic sounds of each word. For example, when you are teaching the word family **–ange** *(range, ranges, arrange, arranges, arrangement, arrangements)* what is important is the teaching of the **–ange** ending, the plural ending and the **–ment** suffix as well as the initial consonant sounds and consonant blends.

Teaching Methodology
- Give each word separately.
- Say the word. Give it in a sentence.
- Let the student(s) attempt the spelling.
- Give the correct spelling. Let each student correct their own spelling. Then give the next word.

Teaching Steps

Using contrasting marker colors will allow your students to more easily recognize the word patterns in each word. For example: when you give the correct spelling of **spinning** write the base **–in** in your base word color. Then, *"double the **n** and add **ing** to get **inning**."* Add **p** and **s** in a contrasting color to get **spinning.**

NOTE: The most common mistake made in teaching *Sequential Spelling* is to give the entire test and then correct it. Students must self correct after each word, not at the end of the test.

Extra practice with homophone lists
At the bottom of each page are lists of homophones (words which sound exactly alike but have different meanings as well as spellings). You may want to include some practice of these concepts in your spelling lessons. Here are a few ideas for teaching homophones:

Homophone Pictionary – Give your student a card with the homophone pair and have them draw pictures of each. The other students can guess the homophones.

Silly Sentences – Give your students a list of homophone pairs and have them come up with silly sentences using the homophone pair.

Homophone Old Maid – Make about twenty pairs of cards with a homophone written on them. Include an "old maid" card as well. Deal the cards as evenly as possible. Then play "Old Maid." When there is a match, have the student show both cards and define EACH word in the homophone pair or use them correctly in a sentence.

ABC Homophone - Have your students come up with twenty-six homophone pairs, one for each letter of the alphabet.

Student Book
The student workbook (available separately from *Wave 3 Learning www.Wave3Learning.com*) has a "Using Your Words" section after each lesson. Students are given brief assignments to stretch their use of the words they have just learned. Four *Story Starter* pages are also included at the back of the book for use as creative writing exercises. The answer key for the student workbook is in this teacher edition. After teaching the day's lesson, you can choose to have your student complete the "Using Your Words" section of their workbook, extend the lesson as described below or move on to another subject.

PROGRESS EVALUATION

Evaluation tests are provided after the 40th, 80th, 120th, 160th and 180th lessons. If you choose to create other tests for grading purposes, they should be given at a separate time and students should be graded on their learning of the spelling of the sounds—not the words.

Administering the Evaluation Tests
Read the tests aloud to your students and ask them to complete the word in the sentence. Initial consonants and blends are given – only the spelling pattern used is tested. Note: If your students are <u>not</u> using the student workbook, you may download the student version of the evaluation tests in pdf format free of charge from the *Sequential Spelling website*, www.SequentialSpelling.com.

ABOUT THE TEACHER TEXT

Notations

* asterisks remind the teacher that the word has a homophone (same pronunciation, different spelling) or heteronym (same spelling, different word and different pronunciation), or does not follow the normal pattern. For example, gyp ** should logically be spelled "jip." Similarly, the word proper ** should logically be spelled "propper" just like hopper, and copper, and stopper, but it is not. Homophones and homographs are listed for your convenience so that you make sure to use the word correctly in a sentence, like "billed. We were billed for extra carpeting. billed" or "build. We will build our house on a hill. build"

Abbreviations   Am = American spelling   Br = British spelling

Words in Bold Print

These are the most commonly used words and the most important to learn. Some words (like doesn't) don't follow regular word patterns and are repeated many times throughout the series. So, you do not have to use all the words in each word list, but please make sure you cover all the words in bold print. At the end of this curriculum, your students should be able to spell the most common words and have learned the most common patterns that occur in words.

Student Handwriting Expectations

Since the students correct their own spelling, they should be expected to write clearly and legibly. The daily tests can and should be used for handwriting practice because the patterns, being repetitive, can be a help in developing legible handwriting. As the teacher, you should set clear standards for acceptable handwriting on these spelling tests.

CUSTOMIZING *SEQUENTIAL SPELLING* FOR YOUR STUDENT

Change the Words on the Tests

You may decide you want to add, change or delete some words on each day's spelling list. Great! If you would prefer to start with a different word family, feel free. *Sequential Spelling* lists most of the words in each family, but not all. We have a supplemental resource, *The Patterns of English Spelling*, which has lists of all the word family patterns used in the series. It is available for purchase from *www.wave3learning.com*.

Give the Test Again

If you decide to give the test again, allow at least two hours between re-tests. We also recommend that the absolute maximum number of times that *Sequential Spelling* tests be given each day is four times.

Increase/Decrease the Pace

Increase the time spent each day on spelling. You could try going through four days of *Sequential Spelling* 1 every day until it is finished and then move through four days of *Sequential Spelling* 2 every day, and continue on through four levels of *Sequential Spelling* in six months.

	1st day	2nd day	3rd day	4th day
1.	freakish	freakishly	freaky	fiendish
2.	ticklish	outlandish	outlandishly	**rubbish**
3.	bluish	blemish	blemishes	**Spanish**
4.	purplish	radish	radishes	**Danish**
5.	blackish	publish	publisher	**British**
6.	whitish	** **polish**	**polishes**	polishing
7.	Swedish	Sweden	**Irish**	two Irishmen
8.	Turkish	Turkey	**Jewish**	sheepish
9.	**English**	Englishman	Englishmen	brackish
10.	** **Polish**	Poland	outlandish	outlandishly
11.	* **parish**	parishes	perishable	perishables
12.	* **perish**	perishes	perished	perishing
13.	childish	childishly	childishness	**students**
14.	**selfish**	selfishly	selfishness	Finland
15.	unselfish	unselfishly	unselfishness	Finns
16.	**foolish**	foolishly	foolishness	* **Finnish**
17.	stylish	stylishly	stylishness	fetish
18.	devilish	devilishly	deviltry	**their** house
19.	impish	impishly	squeamish	**It's** over **there**.
20.	feverish	**solder!**	**solders**	**soldered**
21.	snobbish	snobbishly	**tongue!**	tongues
22.	**finish**	finishes	finished	finishing
23.	**relish**	relishes	relished	relishing
24.	**accomplish**	accomplishes	accomplished	accomplishments
25.	famish	famished	famine	unfinished

*Homophones:
parish/perish A county in Louisiana is called a parish as is a church's congregation.
 To perish is to die or be destroyed.
finish/Finnish Finish your dinner.
 Do you know how to speak Finnish?
relish/relish Here's some pickle relish for your hot dog. She looked forward to graduation with relish.

** Heteronyms:
Polish ("POH lish") The Polish people really know how to polish their shoes.
polish ("PAH lish")

! Insane words:
solder ("SAH dur") The letter l should really be a d, but it isn't. Pronounce the word as if it were spelled "sodder."
tongue "TUNG") The word tongue "TUNG" should be spelled "tung" but it isn't.
wee She called the baby boy a wee lad and the girl a wee lass.
see I can see you.
sea A sea is bigger than a lake; smaller than an ocean.

	5th day	**6th day**	**7th day**	**8th day**
1.	nourish	nourishes	nourishing	nourishment
2.	skirmish	skirmishes	skirmished	skirmishing
3.	banish	banishes	banished	banishing
4.	**vanish**	vanishes	vanished	vanishing
5.	diminish	diminishes	diminished	diminishing
6.	astonish	astonishes	astonished	astonishment
7.	**punish**	**punishes**	**punished**	**punishment**
8.	flourish	flourishes	flourished	flourishing
9.	anguish	anguishes	anguished	anguishing
10.	languish	languishes	languished	languishing
11.	vanquish	vanquishes	vanquished	vanquishing
12.	lavish	lavishes	lavished	lavishly
13.	abolish	abolishes	abolished	abolition
14.	replenish	replenishes	replenished	plentiful
15.	admonish	admonishes	admonished	admonishing
16.	distinguish	distinguishes	distinguished	distinguishing
17.	extinguish	extinguishes	extinguished	extinguisher
18.	relinquish	relinquishes	relinquished	relinquishing
19.	**establish**	**establishes**	**established**	**establishment**
20.	reestablish	reestablishes	reestablished	reestablishing
21.	embellish	embellishes	embellished	embellishment
22.	**cabin**	cabins	cabinet	cabinetry
23.	**robin**	robins	paraffin	elfin
24.	griffin	griffins	muffin	**muffins**
25.	**coffin**	coffins	ragamuffin	ragamuffins

*Homophones:

sees   She sees everything that happens in our neighborhood.

seas   Lakes are smaller than seas. Oceans are bigger.

seize   The police wanted to seize my uncle's car.

flee   To flee is to run away.

flea   A flea is a little insect that lives on animals.

flees   A flea flees from insecticide.

fleas   Fleas flee from insecticide.

levy/levee   The state decided to levy a tax to pay for the building of a levee.

	9th day	10th day	11th day	12th day
1.	noggin	noggins	penguin	penguins
2.	origin	origins	original	originally
3.	margin	margins	marginal	marginally
4.	urchin	urchins	toxin	toxins
5.	dolphin	dolphins	intoxicate	intoxication
6.	napkin	napkins	insulin	penicillin
7.	bumpkin	bumpkins	Martin	Martin's friends
8.	pumpkin	pumpkins	gelatin	**soldering!** gun
9.	doeskin	doeskins	hairpin	hairpins
10.	pigskin	pigskins	Austin	Austin's police
11.	goblin	goblins	sequin	sequins
12.	smidgin	smidgins	Cousin Mary	my cousin's car
13.	violin	violins	**soldier!**	soldiers!
14.	Berlin	Berliner	solid	**solidly**
15.	Merlin	Merlin's magic	tongue	tongues
16.	vitamin	vitamins	vital	vitality
17.	basin	basins	second	seconds
18.	moccasin	moccasins	moccasin	moccasins
19.	**raisin**	raisins	**There's** nothing.	**Their** cat died.
20.	assassin	assassins	assassination	assassinations
21.	assassinate	assassinates	assassinated	assassinating
22.	* cousin	cousins	my cousin's car	**They're** not home.
23.	Latin	pectin	That's **theirs**.	We were **there**.
24.	satin	satins	**They're** coming.	We **used to** go **there**.
25.	bulletin	bulletins	**It's too** bad.	**You're supposed to** go.

* Homophones:

These will be repeated throughout the year:

there/their/they're

we're/were

you're/your

! Insane words:

soldier ("SOH'l jur")	A soldier may die in battle.
solder ("SAH dur")	We use solder to fasten wires together.
solid ("SAH lid")	The opposite of hollow is solid.
solider ("SAH lid ur")	If a lid is more solid than its container, it would be solider.
tongue ("Tung")	Stick out your tongue and say "ah."

	13th day	14th day	15th day	16th day
1.	**husband**	husbands	Poland	Poland's
2.	brigand	brigands	Roland	Roland's
3.	midland	midlands	garland	garlands
4.	Midland	Midland's	**island!**	**islands**
5.	Newfoundland	Newfoundland's	*** isle!**	**isles**
6.	woodland	woodlands	*** aisle!**	**aisles**
7.	Iceland	Iceland's	Shetland	Portland
8.	Ireland	Ireland's	Maryland	Maryland's
9.	England	England's	errand	errands
10.	Holland	Holland's	thousand	thousands
11.	Greenland	Greenland's	industry	industries
12.	**legend**	legends	legendary	industrial
13.	stipend	stipends	reverence	industrialist
14.	reverend	reverends	reverent	reverently
15.	**thing**	**things**	infantry	gallantry
16.	anything	**something**	**nothing**	**everything**
17.	starling	starlings	duckling	ducklings
18.	yearling	yearlings	fledgling	fledglings
19.	poetry	paltry	forestry	geometry
20.	sultry	enter	tapestry	tapestries
21.	pantry	entry	sentry	**country**
22.	pantries	entries	sentries	**countries**
23.	gantry	entrance	carpentry	My **country's** flag
24.	gantries	gentry	**winter#**	register
25.	poetry	bigotry	wintry	registry

*Homophones:

isle/I'll/aisle   I'll walk down the aisle on the isle of Capri.

! Insane words:

isle ("YH'l"); island ("YH lund"); aisle; nothing ("NUH thing")

\# Note: The letter E drops when words such as enter and winter change to entry and wintry. The -try and -tries endings sound exactly like tree and trees!

	17th day	18th day	19th day	20th day
1.	daub	daubs	daubed	daubing
2.	dauber	daubers	bauble	baubles
3.	**fraud**	frauds	fraudulent	**applause**
4.	defraud	defrauds	defrauded	defrauding
5.	laud	lauds	lauded	lauding
6.	**applaud**	applauds	**applauded**	applauding
7.	maraud	marauds	marauded	marauding
8.	marauder	marauders	Aunt Maud	Auntie Maude
9.	pedlar	pedlars	peddler	peddlers
10.	beggar	beggars	**peculiar**	peculiarity
11.	cedar	cedars	*** friar**	friars
12.	*** liar**	liars	molar	molars
13.	vulgar	pliers	polar	polarity
14.	**hangar**	hangars	solar	**soldering!** gun
15.	**sugar**	sugars	**popular**	**popularity**
16.	burglar	burglars	burglary	burglaries
17.	**similar**	similarly	similarity	similarities
18.	**cellar***	cellars	spectacular	spectacle
19.	pillar	pillars	particular#	**particularly**
20.	caterpillar	caterpillars	perpendicular	**circle**
21.	**collar**	collars	circular	circularity
22.	scholar	scholars	scholarship	scholarships
23.	cheddar	vinegar	muscular	**muscle**
24.	calendar	calendars	**regular**	regularity
25.	**familiar**	familiarity	irregular	regulations

*Homophones:

liar/lyre	What do you call a dishonest harp? A liar lyre.
friar/frier/fryer	What do you call a monk that fries chicken? A frier friar or a fryer friar.
cellar/seller	What do you call a basement salesman? A cellar seller.
peddler/pedlar	Peddler is the American spelling. Pedlar is typically British.

! Insane Word:

soldering ("SAH'd dur ing")

Note: The letter u jumps up and inserts itself between the letters c and l in words that end -cle while the e drops with an -ar ending. *Particle* becomes *particular*, *circle* becomes *circular*, *muscle* becomes *muscular*, etc.

	21st day	22nd day	23rd day	24th day
1.	**angle#**	**single**	**triangle**	**rectangle**
2.	**angular**	**singular**	**triangular**	**rectangular**
3.	jugular	lunar	lunacy	lunatic
4.	***** altar	altars	tartar	mortar
5.	Gibraltar	nectar	bursar	Caesar
6.	**method**	methods	methodical	methodically
7.	**period**	periods	periodical	periodically
8.	medic	medics	**public**	republic
9.	medical	medically	publications	Republican
10.	**medicine**	medicinal	***** **symbol**	symbols
11.	**traffic**	garlic	symbolic	symbolism
12.	pacify	pacifies	alcoholic	alcoholism
13.	pacific	Pacific Ocean	stomach	stomach ache
14.	specify	specifies	specified	specifying
15.	specific	specifically	specifications	species
16.	terrify	terrifies	**terrified**	**terrifying**
17.	terrific	terrifically	terror	**It's** over **there.**
18.	science	sciences	**They're** coming.	**There's** a reason.
19.	scientist	scientists	That is **theirs**.	**Their** son won.
20.	scientific	scientifically	unscientific	unscientifically
21.	**magic**	magical	magically	**magician**
22.	**music**	musical	musically	**musician**
23.	**electric**	electrical	electrically	**electrician**
24.	tragic	tragically	**tragedy**	tragedies
25.	strategic	strategically	strategy	strategies

*Homophones:

altar/alter   The minister decided to alter the altar as part of the church alterations.
symbol/cymbal   What do you call a sign for a clashing sound? A cymbal symbol.

Note: The letter *u* jumps up and inserts itself between the letters *g* and *l* in words that end *-gle* while the e drops with an *-ar* ending. *Angle* becomes *angular*, *triangle* becomes *triangular*, etc.

	25th day	**26th day**	**27th day**	**28th day**
1.	**picnic**	picnics	**picnicked**	**picnicking**
2.	**panic**	panics	**panicked**	**panicking**
3.	**mimic**	mimics	**mimicked**	**mimicking**
4.	comic	comics	comical	comically
5.	economy	economies	economize	economizing
6.	economic	economical	economically	economist
7.	academy	academies	atomic	dynamite
8.	academic	cosmic	dynamic	dynamo
9.	**clinic**	clinics	clinical	clinically
10.	organic	inorganic	hectic	static
11.	**mechanic**	mechanics	mechanical	mechanically
12.	**ocean**!	citric acid	**drama**	dramas
13.	oceanic	nitric acid	**dramatic**	dramatically
14.	* **scene**	gastric acid	**fanatic**	fanatically
15.	scenic	lyre	**frantic**	frantically
16.	ethnic	lyric	lyrics	lyrical
17.	**hero**	diplomacy	diplomat	diplomatic
18.	heroic	heroically	heroism	diplomatically
19.	topic	topical	**Arctic**	Antarctic
20.	**tropic**	tropics	tropical	Antarctica
21.	**fabric**	fabrics	diabetic	diabetes
22.	* **base**	**basis**	apology	apologies
23.	**basic**	basically	apologetic	**apologize**#
24.	* **centre**	egocentric	obstetrics	obstetrician
25.	centric	eccentric	physics	**physician**

* Homophones:

base/bass   What do you call a real low-down singer? A base bass.

seen/scene   What's a part of a play you just saw? A seen scene.

centre/center   When Americans want to fancy up the name of a center they use the British

spelling *centre*.

! Insane Word:

ocean ("OH shun")   The letters ce form the "sh" digraph and the letters –an are pronounced "un" just as in Americ*an*, Canadi*an*, tobogg*an*, etc.

_____
Note: In British English it's –ise instead of –ize. British never apologize, but they do apologise.

	29th day	30th day	31st day	32nd day
1.	**surface**	surfaces	surfaced	surfacing
2.	preface	prefaces	prefaced	prefacing
3.	palace	palaces	**necklace**	necklaces
4.	**furnace**	furnaces	terrace	terraces
5.	menace	menaces	menaced	menacing
6.	solace	Wallace	populace	populace
7.	**sauce**	sauces	**saucer**	saucers
8.	saucy	applesauce	saucier	sauciest
9.	* **peace**	peaceful	**peacefully**	peaceable
10.	peacetime	**peacemaker**	peace officer	peace offering
11.	* **Greece**	Greece's people	Greeks	fleecy
12.	fleece	fleeces	fleeced	fleecing
13.	deuce	deuces	deuced	deucing
14.	**office**	offices	**officer**	officers
15.	**service**	**services**	serviced	servicing
16.	disservice	justice	justices	malice
17.	**notice**	notices	noticed	noticing
18.	**practice**	practices	practiced	practicing
19.	apprentice	apprentices	apprenticed	apprenticing
20.	**prejudice**	prejudices	prejudiced	prejudicing
21.	**Alice**	Alice's car	chalice	chalices
22.	Janice	Janice's place	Venice	Venice's canals
23.	accomplice	accomplices	novice	novices
24.	armistice	armistices	cowardice	injustice
25.	**promise**	**promises**	**promised**	**promising**

***Homophones**:

peace/piece   A piece of pie can give peace of mind.

Greece/grease   What do you call Greek oil? Greece grease.

! Insane Words:

Anchor ("ANG kur"); Nice ("NEE-ss"); island; stomach ("STUM ik")

Note: In British English –ize words are spelled –ise. The British specialise and Americans specialize

	33rd day	**34th day**	**35th day**	**36th day**
1.	**grocer**	grocers	grocery	groceries
2.	**juice**	juices	juicy	juiciest
3.	sluice	sluices	sluiced	sluicing
4.	**police**	polices	policed	policing
5.	policeman	policemen	policewoman	policewomen
6.	caprice	caprices	Denice	Denice's nephew
7.	Bernice	Bernice's niece	* **Nice**, France!	Clarice
8.	Felice	Felice's daughter	Denise	Denise's
9.	police work	* **Greece**	valise	valises
10.	* **grease**	greases	greased	greasing
11.	**such**	much too fast	**anchor!**	* **anchors!**
12.	mulch	mulches	mulched	mulching
13.	gulch	gulches	**stomach!**	stomach ache
14.	dry-gulch	dry-gulches	dry-gulched	dry-gulching
15.	**special**	specials	specialty	specialties
16.	**specialize#**	specializes	specialized	specializing
17.	especial	especially	**racial**	racially
18.	**social**	socially	**official**	officials
19.	commercial	commercials	commercially	noncommercial
20.	crucial	crucially	facial	facials
21.	artificial	artificially	unofficial	unofficially
22.	beneficial	beneficially	judicial	sacrificial
23.	antisocial	provincial	judicious	* **They're** going.
24.	glacier	glaciers	prejudicial	**island!**
25.	suspicion	suspicions	suspicious	suspiciously

*Homophones:

lGreece/greaseWhat's Greek oil? Greece grease.

Nice/niece   What do you call my nephew's sister who lives in Nice, France? My Nice niece.

there/their/they'reThey're building their house over there.

! Insane Words:

Anchor ("ANG kur"); Nice ("NEE-ss"); island; stomach ("STUM ik")

Note: In British English –ize words are spelled –ise. The British specialise and Americans specialize

	37th day	38th day	39th day	40th day
1.	**lock**	* **locks**	locked	locking
2.	unlock	unlocks	unlocked	unlocking
3.	padlock	padlocks	padlocked	lockers
4.	**clock**	clocks	clocked	clocking
5.	nine **o'clock**	blocks	blocked	blocking
6.	flock	flocks	blocker	blockers
7.	cock	cocks	cocked	cocking
8.	peacock	peacocks	cocky	cockiest
9.	**rock**	rocks	rocked	rocking
10.	crock	crocks	rocky	rockiest
11.	**knock**	knocks	knocked	knocking
12.	**sock**	* **socks**	socked	socking
13.	**stock**	stocks	stocked	stocking
14.	mock	mocks	mocked	mocking
15.	smock	smocks	hockey	anchored
16.	hock	hocks	hocked	hocking
17.	* **dock**	* **docks**	docked	docking
18.	frock	frocks	cameo	cameos
19.	defrock	defrocks	defrocked	defrocking
20.	shock	shocks	shocked	shocking
21.	duck	* **ducks**	* **ducked**	ducking
22.	**luck**	lucks	lucky	luckiest
23.	cluck	clucks	clucked	clucking
24.	pluck	plucks	plucked	plucking
25.	**buck**	bucks	bucked	bucking

* Homophones:

lock/lox/loch   Don't forget to lock the door.
   A Scotsman calls a lake a loch.
   Ask for lox at a deli and you'll get salmon.

socks/sox   Some people wear socks. Others wear sox.
ducked/duct   We ducked under the awning to escape the rain.
   My dad's company does air duct cleaning.

Sequential Spelling Level 4 - Teacher's Guide

Evaluation Test #1 (After 40 Days)

		Pattern being tested	Lesson word is in
1.	We have some unfin**ished** business to attend to.	ished	4
2.	Every house should have a fire extingu**isher**.	isher	8
3.	Do you like bran muff**ins**?	ins	8
4.	You should try walking in another's moccas**ins***.	ins	12
5.	Would you like an en**try** level job?	try	14
6.	The English brought star**lings** to America.	lings	14
7.	Speakers love appl**ause**.	ause	20
8.	No one likes to be defr**auded**.	auded	19
9.	I wish you wouldn't be so part**icular**.	icular	19
10.	Famili**arity** breeds contempt.	arity	18
11.	Please give at least one spec**ific** example.	ific	21
12.	My older sister is an electri**cian**.	cian	24
13.	My older brother is a musi**cian**.	cian	24
14.	We told him not to panic, but he still pan**icked**.	ked	27
15.	Afterwards, he was very apolo**getic**.	etic	27
16.	Have you not**iced** how quickly you're learning?	iced	31
17.	A teacher spe**cial**izes in helping people learn.	cial	34
18.	It is cru**cial** that you learn certain spelling concepts.	cial	33
19.	It will prove benefi**cial** if you can master them.	cial	33
20.	Careful watching of commer**cials** can help your reading.	cial	34

*This word was never given, but another form of the word was used.

	41st day	42nd day	43rd day	44th day
1.	muck	mucks	mucked	mucking
2.	puck	pucks	Anchorage, AK	**headache**
3.	chuck	chucks	chucked	chucking
4.	woodchuck	woodchucks	Chuck's name	**stuck**
5.	suck	sucks	sucked	sucking
6.	**truck**	trucks	trucked	trucking
7.	**struck**	Huck Finn	trucker	truckers
8.	article	articles	circular	**particular**
9.	**particle**	**particles**	**circus**	**particularly**
10.	**circle**	circles	circled	circling
11.	encircle	encircles	encircled	encircling
12.	**uncle**	uncles	**Uncle** Tim	my **uncle's** house
13.	**icicle**	icicles	**vehicle**	vehicles
14.	**bicycle**	bicycles	**vehicular**	**cameo**
15.	tricycle	tricycles	**biscuit**	**biscuits**
16.	* **muscle**	muscles	**muscular**	muscularity
17.	**miracle**	miracles	**miraculous**	miraculously
18.	**spectacle**	spectacles	**spectacular**	spectacularly
19.	obstacle	obstacles	debacle	debacles
20.	manacle	manacles	manacled	manacling
21.	oracle	oracles	oracular	**islands**
22.	act	* **acts**	acted	acting
23.	actor	actors	active	**action**
24.	enact	enacts	enacted	enacting
25.	re-enact	re-enacts	re-enacted	re-enacting

* **Homophones:**
muscle/mussel What do you call clam-like strength? Mussel muscle.
acts/ax/axe What do you call it when a hatchet goes on stage? The ax acts.

	45th day	46th day	47th day	48th day
1.	**fact**	***facts**	faction	factions
2.	factor	factors	factored	factoring
3.	***tract**	***tracts**	tractor	tractors
4.	**attract**	attracts	attracted	attracting
5.	attractor	attractive	**attraction**	attractions
6.	distract	distracts	distracted	distracting
7.	tractor	tractors	distraction	distractions
8.	abstract	abstracts	abstraction	abstracting
9.	extract	extracts	extracted	extraction
10.	detract	detracts	detracting	detraction
11.	retract	retracts	retracted	retraction
12.	**subtract**	subtracts	subtracting	**subtraction**
13.	refract	refracts	refracting	refraction
14.	****con**tract	**con**tracts	con<u>tract</u>ed	con<u>tract</u>ing
15.	******con**tract**	con**tracts**	con<u>tract</u>ed	con<u>tract</u>ing
16.	**con**tractor	**con**tractors	con<u>tract</u>ion	con<u>tract</u>ions
17.	***pact**	pacts	cataract	cataracts
18.	**com**pact	**com**pacts	comp<u>act</u>or	compactors
19.	compact	com**pacts**	comp<u>act</u>ed	comp<u>act</u>ing
20.	impact	impacts	impacted	impacting
21.	**exact**	exacts	exacted	exacting
22.	***tact**	***tacts**	tactic	tactics
23.	**character**	characters	characteristic	characteristics
24.	connecter	connecters	characteristically	uncharacteristically
25.	**fracture**	fractures	fractured	fracturing

* **Homophones:**

pact/packed   They signed a peace pact. They packed up their belongings.
tract/tracked   The dogs tracked the fox to a large tract of swamp land.
tact/tacked   They tried a new tact. They tacked up a poster.

** **Heteronyms:**

contract/contract   You sign a **con**tract. You con**tract** a disease.
compact/compact   To com**pact** is to make small. A **com**pact is small.

	49th day	50th day	51st day	52nd day
1.	**direct**	directs	directed	directing
2.	director	directors	directive	**directions**
3.	erect	erects	erected	erecting
4.	**correct**	corrects	corrected	correcting
5.	incorrect	correctly	corrective	**correction**
6.	** **per**fect	**per**fectly	perfective	**perfection**
7.	** per**fect**	per**fect**s	perfected	perfecting
8.	infect	infects	infected	**infection**
9.	* **affect**	affects	affecting	**affection**
10.	* **effect**	effects	effective	effectively
11.	**defect**	defects	defective	defection
12.	**dejected**	dejection	reject	**rejection**
13.	inject	injection	**cello!**	cello
14.	** **obj**ect	**obj**ects	**objective**	objectively
15.	** ob**ject**	ob**ject**s	objected	**objection**
16.	** **pro**ject	**pro**jects	projector	**projection**
17.	** pro**ject**	pro**ject**s	projected	projecting
18.	** **sub**ject	**sub**jects	subjective	subjection
19.	** sub**ject**	sub**ject**s	subjected	subjecting
20.	**elect**	elects	elected	electing
21.	elector	electors	elective	**election**
22.	**select**	selects	selected	selecting
23.	selector	selectors	selective	**selection**
24.	intellect	intellects	intelligent	intelligence
25.	**neglect**	neglects	neglected	neglecting

* **Homophones:**

affect/effect: The most Effective way we have found to teach the difference is by using the THE test. Whenever you can put the word the before "uh FEK't" spell it effect. Otherwise spell it affect.

** **Heteronyms:**

object/object: I object ("ub JEK't") to being the object ("AH'b jekt") of ridicule.
perfect/perfect: I want to perfect ("pur FEK't") my technique. Then I'll be perfect.
project/project: I don't project ("proh JEK't") my voice. I finished my project ("PRAH jekt").
subject/subject: Don't subject ("sub JEK't") me to being the subject ("SUB jekt") of an article.

! **Insane Word:**

The "c" in cello is pronounced as a CH sound, "CHello."

	53rd day	54th day	55th day	56th day
1.	reflect	* **reflects**	reflected	reflecting
2.	reflector	reflectors	reflective	reflections
3.	deflect	deflects	deflected	deflection
4.	inflect	inflects	inflective	inflection
5.	genuflect	genuflects	genuflecting	genuflection
6.	**expect**	expects	**expected**	expecting
7.	retrospect	disrespect	**unexpected**	**expectations**
8.	**respect**	respects	respected	respective
9.	**inspect**	inspects	inspected	inspecting
10.	inspector	inspectors	inspection	inspections
11.	prospect	prospects	prospected	prospecting
12.	prospector	prospectors	prospective	suspicious
13.	** **sus**pect	**sus**pects	suspicion	suspicions
14.	** sus**pect**	sus**pects**	suspected	suspecting
15.	sect	* **sects**	section	dissection
16.	dissect	dissects	dissected	dissecting
17.	bisect	bisects	bisecting	bisection
18.	intersect	intersects	intersected	intersection
19.	architect	architects	architecture	detective
20.	**detect**	detects	detected	detecting
21.	**protect**	protects	protected	protecting
22.	hectic	hectically	protective	**protection**
23.	**electric**	electrical	electrically	electrician
24.	electricity	**insect**	**insects**	imperfect
25.	lecture	lectures	lectured	lecturing

*Homophones:

sex/sects What do you call exclusively male or female religions? Sex sects.

reflex/reflects What do you call the automatic bounces of light waves? The reflects reflex.

** Heteronyms:

suspect/suspect I suspect ("suh SPEK't") that he knew the suspect ("SUS spek't") personally.

	57th day	58th day	59th day	60th day
1.	**strict**	strictly	restrictive	restrictions
2.	restrict	restricts	restricted	restricting
3.	constrict	constricts	constricted	constricting
4.	**district**	districts	constrictive	constrictions
5.	** <u>ad</u>dict	<u>ad</u>dicts	addictive	addiction
6.	** ad<u>**dict**</u>	ad<u>dicts</u>	addicted	addicting
7.	**predict**	predicts	predicted	predicting
8.	predictor	predictors	predictive	prediction
9.	edict	edicts	contradiction	contradictions
10.	**contradict**	contradicts	contradicted	contradicting
11.	Benedict	Benedict's	benediction	benedictions
12.	interdict	interdicts	interdicted	interdicting
13.	**indict!**	indicts	indicted	indicting
14.	** <u>con</u>vict	<u>con</u>victs	conviction	convictions
15.	** con<u>**vict**</u>	con<u>victs</u>	convicted	convicting
16.	evict	evicts	evicted	evicting
17.	afflict	afflicts	afflicted	afflicting
18.	derelict	derelicts	**cello**	**cello**
19.	depict	depicts	depicted	depicting
20.	* **picture**	pictures	pictured	picturing
21.	* **pitcher**	pitchers	pitching	pitches
22.	concoct	concocts	concocted	concocting
23.	**doctor**	doctors	doctored	concoction
24.	proctor	proctors	proctored	proctoring
25.	Victor	**Victoria**	**victory**	**victori**ous

* **Homophones:**

pitcher/picture — What do you call a photo of a hurler? A pitcher picture. Note: We know that picture **should** be pronounced "PIK chur" as opposed to pitcher ("PICH ur"). However, enough people mispronounce the word that we list it as a homophone so you can play with them if you desire.

** **Heteronyms:**

addict/addict — An addict ("AD dik't") should not try to addict ("uh DIK't") someone else.

convict/convict — Yes, you can convict ("kun VIK't") a convict ("KAH'n vik't") of a crime.

! **Insane Words:**

indict ("in DYH't") — You would think that indict would be spelled "indight" or "indite" but it isn't. Since the root **dict** helps us understand the meaning, we have never changed the spelling as we did the pronunciation.

	61st day	62nd day	63rd day	64th day
1.	** con**duct**	conducts	conducted	conducting
2.	** **con**duct	conductors	conductive	conduction
3.	deduct	deducts	deducted	deducting
4.	deductive	deductively	deduction	deductions
5.	deduce	deduces	deduced	deducing
6.	induce	induces	induced	inducing
7.	inductive	inductively	induction	inductions
8.	induct	inducts	inducted	inducting
9.	abduct	abducts	abducted	abduction
10.	pr**o**duct	pr**o**ducts	pr**o**ductive	pr**o**duction
11.	** pro**duce**	produces	produced	producing
12.	** **pro**duce	viaducts	producer	producers
13.	instruct	instructs	instructed	instructing
14.	instructor	instructors	instructive	instructions
15.	con**struct**	con**structs**	constructed	constructing
16.	**con**struct	**con**structs	constructive	construction
17.	obstruct	obstructs	obstructed	obstruction
18.	* **duct**	* **ducts**	doodler	doodlers
19.	noodle	noodles	poodle	poodles
20.	doodle	doodles	doodled	doodling
21.	* **wood**	woods	wooden	woodenly
22.	* **would**	would	wouldn't	wouldn't
23.	stood	withstood	understood	misunderstood
24.	redwoods	hardwood	plywood	dogwood
25.	good	goods	hard goods	soft goods

* **Homophones:**

duct/ducked — A heat duct carries hot air from a furnace. The batter ducked a wild pitch.

ducts/ducks/duck's/ducks' — Donald Duck ducks ducts. Will a duck's tear ducts produce tears?

would/wood — What would happen if a woodchuck would chuck wood?

25

	65th day	66th day	67th day	68th day
1.	hood	hoods	hooded	hooding
2.	statehood	**falsehood**	falsehoods	sainthood
3.	**manhood**	**womanhood**	**fatherhood**	**motherhood**
4.	**brotherhood**	**sisterhood**	boyhood	girlhood
5.	**childhood**	**likelihood**	**neighborhood**	neighborhoods
6.	**flood**	floods	flooded	flooding
7.	**blood**	bloody	**Beethoven**!	**Beethoven**!
8.	fluid	fluids	**splendid**	splendidly
9.	valid	validly	validity	pyramid
10.	** **invalid**	invalidly	invalidity	stupidly
11.	Druid	Druids	**stupid**	stupidity
12.	* **rude**	**crude**	prude	prudes
13.	**dude**	dudes	duded	duding
14.	elude	eludes	eluded	eluding
15.	nude	nudes	illusive	**illusion**
16.	elude	eludes	eluded	eluding
17.	**attitude**#	attitudes	elusive	elusion
18.	allude	alludes	alluded	allusion
19.	delude	deludes	deluded	**delusion**
20.	intrude	intruders	intrusive	intrusion
21.	protrude	protrudes	protruded	protrusion
22.	extrude	extrudes	extruded	extrusion
23.	include	including	inclusive	inclusion
24.	conclude	concluding	conclusive	**conclusion**
25.	**altitude**#	altitudes	multitude	multitudes

* Homophones:

rude/rued   The carpenter rued the day he was rude.

** Heteronyms:

invalid ("in VAL id")/invalid ("IN vuh lid") Can an invalid be invalid?

! Insane word: Beethoven ("BAY toh vun")

 # Tricky Words: attitude / altitude

Sequential Spelling Level 4 - Teacher's Guide

	69th day	70th day	71st day	72nd day
1.	* **climb**	climbs	climbed	climbing
2.	**limb**	limbs	climber	climbers
3.	**comb**	combs	combed	combing
4.	**tomb**	tombs	tombstone	tombstones
5.	**womb**	wombs	* **lamb**	lambs
6.	**thumb**	thumbs	thumbed	thumbing
7.	**crumb**	crumbs	bomber	bombers
8.	* **bomb**	bombs	bombed	bombing
9.	**dumb**	dumber	dumbest	dumb
10.	**debt**	debts	debtor	debtors
11.	* **gnat**	gnats	leprechaun	leprechauns
12.	gnaw	gnaws	gnawed	gnawing
13.	gnarl	gnarls	gnarled	gnarling
14.	* **gnome**	gnomes	***gnu**	***gnus**
15.	* **sign**	signs	signature	signing
16.	**design**	designs	designation	designing
17.	* **align**	aligns	aligned	alignment
18.	malign	maligns	malignant	malignancy
19.	* **deign**	deigns	deigned	deigning
20.	* **reign**	reigns	reigned	reigning
21.	**foreign**	foreigner	foreigners	**They're** all right.
22.	alm	alms	qualms	They won **their** case.
23.	**palm**	palms	palmed	palming
24.	**calm**	calms	calmed	calming
25.	psalm	psalms	salmon	**salve#**

* Homophones:

climb/clime	Go climb a tree. Find a better climate or clime. Your choice.
bomb/balm	What do you call an ointment that doesn't work? A balm bomb.
gnat/Nat	Nat swallowed a gnat.
lamb/lam	Mary's lamb was on the lam.
gnu/new/knew	I knew the new gnu would get homesick.
gnus/news	No gnus is bad news for a zoo.
gnome/Nome	What do you call an Alaskan dwarf? A Nome gnome.
sign/sine	Knowing what a sine is is a sign of a mathematician.
align/a line	What do you call making a line parallel? To align a line.
Dane/deign	Will the Dane deign to eat an American Danish?
rain/reign/rein	During Elizabeth's reign they had to rein in Walter when it began to rain.

	73rd day	74th day	75th day	76th day
1.	**answer**!	answers	answered	answering
2.	**who**!	who's	* **whose!** book	**They're too** fast.
3.	* **sword**!	swords	swordfish	swordfight
4.	* **wrap**!	* **wraps**	* **wrapped**	wrapping
5.	* **wring**!	* **wrings**	* **wrung**	* **wringing**
6.	**wreck**!	* **wrecks**	wrecked	wrecking
7.	**wrecker**!	wreckers	wren	wrens
8.	**wrath**!	wrathful	* **whole**!	* **wholly**
9.	**wreath**!	wreaths	**wrist**!	wrists
10.	**wren**!	wrens	**writ**!	writs
11.	**wrench**!	wrenches	wrenched	wrenching
12.	**wrestle**!	wrestles	wrestled	wrestling
13.	**wrestler**!	wrestlers	**wrong**!	wrongs
14.	**wrinkle**!	**wrinkles**	**wrinkled**	wrinkling
15.	**write**!	**writes**	**written**	**writing**
16.	writer!	writers	**salve**#	**It's too** easy.
17.	**wright**!	**wrights**	wrought	Edmund Cartwright
18.	writhe!	writhes	writhed	writhing
19.	**grease**	greases	greased	greasing
20.	**lease**	leases	* **leased**	leasing
21.	**release**	releases	released	releasing
22.	cease	ceases	ceased	deceased
23.	crease	**creases**	creased	creasing
24.	**increase**	increases	increased	increasing
25.	**decrease**	decreases	decreased	decreasing

*Homophones:

who's/whose	Who's going to help with whose homework?
rap/wrap	What do you call the end of Hammer's recording session? A rap wrap.
rapped/rapt/wrapped	Hammer rapped. The audience was rapt. We wrapped it up.
ring/wring	You can wring a chicken's neck or put a ring on a finger.
rung/wrung	Jack wrung his hands when he broke a rung on his dad's ladder.
Rex/wrecks	Rex gets into too many wrecks.
whole/hole	What do you call a complete void? A whole hole.
wholly/holy	What do you call completely religious? Wholly holy.
right/write/rite/wright	Bruce Wright should always write a rite right.
Greece/grease	What do you call olive oil? Greece grease.
leased/least	At least he leased a decent car.
sword/soared	What happened when King Arthur threw Excalibur? The sword soared.

!Insane Words: Notice the w is silent in these words.

Note: Salve is pronounced ("SAV.") The l is silent.

	77th day	78th day	79th day	80th day
1.	**sweat**	sweats	**sweater**	sweating
2.	**threat**	threats	**They're** crazy.	sweaters
3.	**threaten**	threatens	threatened	threatening
4.	* **favor**	favors	favored	favoring
5.	* **favour**	favours	favoured	favouring
6.	* **favorable**	favorably	**favorite**	favorites
7.	* **favourable**	favourably	**favourite**	favourites
8.	* **flavor**	flavors	flavored	flavoring
9.	* **flavour**	flavours	flavoured	flavouring
10.	* **savor**	savors	savored	savoring
11.	* **savour**	savours	savoured	savouring
12.	* **saviour**	saviours	**savior**	saviors
13.	**deaf**	deafen	deafens	deafening
14.	**beef**	beefs	beefed	beefing
15.	beefy	beefier	beefiest	reef
16.	**leave**	leaves	**left**	leaving
17.	cleave	cleaves	cleft/cleaved	cleaving
18.	cleaver	cleavers	weaver	weavers
19.	heave	heaves	heaved	heaving
20.	weave	weaves	weaved	weaving
21.	bereave	bereaves	bereft/bereaved	bereaving
22.	**heavy**	heavier	heaviest	heavily
23.	heavyweight	heavyweights	Their boss left.	He went **there, too.**
24.	**sleeve**	sleeves	They're not there.	**Their** dog went **there**.
25.	re**cei**ve!	re**cei**ves	re**cei**ved	re**cei**ving

* **Homophones:** *The following homophones ending in -or are standard American spellings. Those ending in -our are standard British spellings.*

favor/favour	labor/labour	vigor/vigour	armor/amour
favorable/favourable	neighbor/neighbour	behavior/behaviour	humor/humour
flavor/flavour	harbor/harbour	valor/valour	rumor/rumour
savor/savour	rancor/rancour	color/colour	tumor/turmour
savior/saviour	ardor/ardour	parlor/parlour	honor/honour
	odor/odour	clamor/clamour	vapor/vapour
	rigor/rigour	glamour/glamour	fervor/fervour

Note: Remember the rule – "I before e, except after c."

29

Evaluation Test #2 (After 80 Days)

		Pattern being tested	Lesson word is in
1.	It would be a mir**acle** if Chicago won the series.	acle	41
2.	The patient made a mir**aculous** recovery.	aculous	43
3.	The two countries signed a non-aggression p**act**.	act	45
4.	Sugar attr**acts** ants.	acts	46
5.	Do you like previews of coming attr**actions**?	actions	48
6.	We stand corr**ected**.	ected	51
7.	Do you need dir**ections** on how to get there?	ections	52
8.	You really should wear prot**ective** headgear.	ective	55
9.	We attended three l**ectures** last year.	ectures	54
10.	That patient is on a restr**icted** diet.	icted	59
11.	How many of the psychic's pred**ictions** came true?	ictions	60
12.	How many heat d**ucts** are there in this room?	ucts	62
13.	My brother works for a constr**uction** company.	uction	64
14.	I think my sister has a real attit**ude** problem.	ude	65
15.	How do you think I arrived at that concl**usion**?	usion	68
16.	What would you like inscribed on your t**omb**stone?	omb	71
17.	Have you seen the latest house des**igns**?	igns	70
18.	Our national debt seems to keep incr**easing**.	easing	76
19.	I don't like to be threat**ened** by anyone.	ened	79
20.	We gave them new sw**eaters** for their anniversary.	eaters	80

Sequential Spelling Level 4 – Teacher's Guide

	81st day	82nd day	83rd day	84th day
1.	**receive**	receives	received	receiving
2.	receiver	receivers	receptive	reception
3.	deceive	deceives	deceived	deceiving
4.	receipt	receipts	deceptive	deception
5.	conceive	conceives	conceived	conceiving
6.	concept	concepts	conceivable	conception
7.	misconceive	misconceives	misconceived	misconceiving
8.	inconceivable	inconceivably	ceiling	misconception
9.	preconceive	preconceives	preconceived	preconception
10.	novel	novels	novelty	novelties
11.	grovel	grovels	groveled grovelled!	groveling grovelling
12.	**shovel**	shovels	**shoveled shovelled**	shoveling shovelling
13.	swivel	swivels	swiveled swivelled	swiveling swivelling
14.	shrivel	shrivels	shriveled shrivelled	shriveling shrivelling
15.	snivel	snivels	sniveled snivelled	sniveling snivelling
16.	revel	revels	reveled revelled	reveling revelling
17.	**level**	levels	leveled levelled	leveling levelling
18.	bevel	bevels	beveled bevelled	beveling bevelling
19.	**dreadful**	dreadfully	gleeful	gleefully
20.	spiteful	spitefully	**peaceful**	**peacefully**
21.	**forceful**	forcefully	resourceful	resourcefully
22.	**shameful**	shamefully	**eyeful**	eyefuls
23.	**handful**	handfuls	armful	armfuls
24.	**spoonful**	spoonfuls	**mouthful**	mouthfuls
25.	pocketful	pocketfuls	teaspoonful	teaspoonfuls

! Note: British spellings of these words always double the l; American spellings do not. Either is correct – just instruct your students to be consistent.

	85th day	86th day	87th day	88th day
1.	**helpful**	helpfully	thankful	thankfully
2.	**skillful**	skillfully	harmful	harmfully
3.	**cheerful**	**cheerfully**	powerful	powerfully
4.	**eager**	**eagerly**	eagerness	eagerly
5.	meager	tiger	tigers	meagerly
6.	**cabbage**	cabbages	cribbage	garbage
7.	**courage**	courageous	courageously	encouragement
8.	**encourage**	encourages	encouraged	encouraging
9.	discourage	discourages	discouraged	discouraging
10.	**image**	images	message	messages
11.	**bandage**	bandages	bandaged	bandaging
12.	pilgrimage	orphanage	sausage	sausages
13.	scrimmage	scrimmages	**luggage**	breakage
14.	rummage	vantage	carriage	carriages
15.	mileage	**advantage**	advantages	advantageous
16.	**marriage**	marriages	wreckage	**storage**
17.	**package**	packages	packaged	packaging
18.	**village**	villages	villager	villagers
19.	**damage**	damages	**damaged**	damaging
20.	**manage**	manages	**managed**	**managing**
21.	**manager**	managers	management	passageway
22.	patronage	parsonage	**passage**	passages
23.	**average**	averages	averaged	averaging
24.	percentage	percentages	**shortage**	shortages
25.	hostage	hostages	**language**	languages

\# Note: Words that have just one syllable in their base ending in -age rhyme with age and page. The -age words on this page have more than one syllable in their base and rhyme with the -idge ("ij") words.

	89th day	**90th day**	**91st day**	**92nd day**
1.	**cottage**	cottages	postage	wattage
2.	beverage	beverages	dosage	homage
3.	ravage	ravages	ravaged	ravaging
4.	**college**	colleges	collegiate	college
5.	**privilege**	privileges	privileged	privilege
6.	sacrilege	sacrileges	sacrilegious	sacrilege
7.	**huge**	hugely	Bridget	Bridget's
8.	**ridge**	ridges	ridged	ridging
9.	**bridge**	bridges	bridged	bridging
10.	cartridge	cartridges	midget	midgets
11.	partridge	partridges	widget	widgets
12.	**fudge**	fudges	fudged	fudging
13.	nudge	nudges	nudged	nudging
14.	smudge	smudges	smudged	smudging
15.	grudge	grudges	grudged	grudging
16.	begrudge	begrudges	begrudged	begrudging
17.	budge	budges	budged	budging
18.	**budget**	budgets	budgeted	budgeting
19.	**straight**	straights	straighter	straightest
20.	**straighten**	straightens	straightened	straightening
21.	**laugh**!	laughs	laughed	laughing
22.	**laughter**!	taught	daughter	daughters
23.	**caught**#	fraught	naught	naughty
24.	**slaughter**!	slaughters	slaughtered	slaughtering
25.	**daughter**!	daughters	my daughter's car	my daughters' cars

! Insane Words: laugh ("laff") and laughter ("LAF tur") and daughter ("DAW tur") and *caught* ("KAW't")

Note: In those few dialects that do not distinguish between the "AW" and "AH" vowels, the words cot ("KAH't") and caught ("KAW't") are homophones.

	93rd day	94th day	95th day	96th day
1.	* **weigh**	**weighs**	* **weighed**	weighing
2.	* **weight**	**weights**	weighty	weightiest
3.	* **sleigh**	sleighs	sleighed	sleighing
4.	* **neigh**	neighs	neighed	neighing
5.	**neighbor**	**neighbors**	**neighborhood**	neighborhoods
6.	**eagle**	eagles	bugle	bugles
7.	beagle	beagles	bugler	buglers
8.	regal	regale	**They're** not going.	**Their** dog died.
9.	finagle	finagles	finagled	finagling
10.	inveigle	inveigles	inveigled	inveigling
11.	legal	breaker	broke	breakers
12.	* **break**	breaks	broken	breaking
13.	**breakfast**	breakfasts	freak	freaks
14.	* **steak**	steaks	squeak	squeaks
15.	* **weak**	teak	teakwood	squeaking
16.	**weaken**	weakens	weakened	weakening
17.	beak	beaks	squeaky	squeaked
18.	* **peak**	peaks	leaky	squeakiest
19.	* **leak**	leaks	leaked	leaking
20.	**speak**	speaks	spoke	speaking
21.	speaker	speakers	spoken	streaker
22.	streak	streaks	streaked	streaking
23.	sneak	sneaks	sneaked	sneaking
24.	sneaker	**sneakers**	sneaky	sneakiest
25.	* **creak**	creaks	creaked	creaking

* Homophones:

neighbor/neighbour	British English uses –our in all the neighbour words from neighbouring to neighbourhood.
peak/peek/pique	A peek at a mountain peak might pique your curiosity.
weigh/way/whey	By the way, how much does a bowl of curds and whey weigh.
weighed/wade	You can wade in water. They weighed their dog.
weight/wait	Wait for the correct weight.
sleigh/slay	To kill a sled is to slay a sleigh.
neigh/nay	Horses neigh. They voted nay instead of aye.
steak/stake	I love to eat steak. You can pound a stake into the ground.
break/brake	Give me a break. Step on the brake.
weak/week	A poor seven days is a weak week.
creak/creek	Doors creak. I like to fish in a creek.
leak/leek	A leak (such as gas) can be dangerous. A leek can be eaten.

	97th day	**98th day**	**99th day**	**100th day**
1.	shriek	shrieks	shrieked	shrieking
2.	spook	spooks	spooked	spooking
3.	spooky	spookier	spookiest	gadzooks
4.	eke	ekes	eked	eking
5.	duke	dukes	Luke	Luke's
6.	fluke	flukes	juke box	nuclear
7.	nuke	nukes	nuked	nuking
8.	rebuke	rebukes	rebuked	rebuking
9.	* **haul**	hauls	hauled	hauling
10.	**overhaul**	overhauls	overhauled	overhauling
11.	caterwaul	caterwauls	caterwauled	caterwauling
12.	* **Paul**	Paul's	Saul	Saul's
13.	* **caul**	cauls	cauliflower	Pauline
14.	**fault**	**faults**	faulted	faulting
15.	faulty	faultier	faultiest	faulty
16.	excel	excels	excelled	excelling
17.	lapel	lapels	excellent	excellence
18.	! **Michel**	**Michel's****	**their** choice	**They're great!**
19.	to **rebel**	she rebels	rebelled	rebelling
20.	a **rebel**	two rebels	rebellion	rebellious
21.	repel	repels	repelled	repelling
22.	repulse	repulses	repulsed	repulsive
23.	**compel**	compels	compelled	compelling
24.	**hotel**	hotels	compulsive	compulsion
25.	dispel	dispels	dispelled	dispelling

* **Homophones**:

haul/hall   They had to haul away the garbage from the hall.

caul/call   If you know what a caul is, call me.

Paul/pall   Paul knows what a pall is and has been a pallbearer.

** **Heteronyms**:

rebel ("re BEL")/rebel ("REB'l") A rebel is one who loves to rebel against authority.

! **Insane Word:** Michel ("mee SHELL") is a French name. Do not confuse with Michael ("MY k'l"). Michel is masculine. The feminine is Michelle.

	101st day	102nd day	103rd day	104th day
1.	propel	propels	propelled	propelling
2.	**motel**	motels	propulsive	jet propulsion
3.	expel	expels	expelled	expelling
4.	cartel	cartels	propeller	expulsion
5.	impel	impels	impelled	impelling
6.	pastel	pastels	impulse	impulsive
7.	* **Abel**	Abel's	kennel	kennels
8.	Israel	Israel's	Israelis	Israelites
9.	**Michael**	Michael's	Ishmael	Michael
10.	**label**	labels	**labeled labelled	**labeling labelling
11.	**cancel**	cancels	**canceled cancelled	**canceling cancelling
12.	Marcel	Marcel's	cancellation	cancellations
13.	parcel	parcels	**parceled parcelled	**parceling parcelling
14.	**model**	models	**modeled modelled	**modeling modelling
15.	yodel	yodels	**yodeled yodelled	**yodeling yodelling
16.	citadel	citadels	fidelity	Fidel
17.	infidel	infidels	infidelity	infidelities
18.	**angel**!	angels	angelic	angelically
19.	satchel	satchels	**bushel**	bushels
20.	Ethel	Ethel's	**camel**	camels
21.	**nickel**	nickels	yokel	yokels
22.	**panel**	panels	**paneled panelled	**paneling panelling
23.	**channel**	channels	**chaneled channelled	**chaneling channelling
24.	**flannel**	flannels	* **kernel**	kernels
25.	Lionel	Lionel's	* **colonel**	the **colonel's**

* **Homophones:**

able/Abel   When Cain's brother was healthy, he was called able Abel.

kernel/colonel   One kernel of corn refused to pop. The colonel threw it out.

** **Heteronyms:**

These heteronyms can be spelled without doubling the -l which is the usual American spelling. But, many American writers are following the British spelling and double the -l. When the -el carries the accent as in compel, excel, and dispel the letter l **must** be doubled.

! **Tricky Word:**   angel ("AY'n jul") Do you have a guardian angel?

angle ("ANG gul") Do you know what a right angle is?

	105th day	106th day	107th day	108th day
1.	Col. Brown	Colonel Brown	colonels	colonel
2.	**tunnel**	tunnels	tunneled tunnelled	tunneling tunnelling
3.	funnel	funnels	funneled funnelled	funneling funnelling
4.	shrapnel	sentinel	sentinels	dorsal fin
5.	chapel	chapels	chaplain	chaplains
6.	scalpel	scalpels	gospel	gospels
7.	**barrel**	barrels	barreled barrelled	barreling barrelling
8.	scoundrel	scoundrels	mongrel	mongrels
9.	**quarrel**	quarrels	quarreled quarrelled	quarrelling
10.	squirrel	squirrels	squirreled squirrelled	squirreling squirrelling
11.	wastrel	wastrels	minstrel	minstrels
12.	apparel	doggerel	easel	easels
13.	diesel	diesels	weasel	weasels
14.	chisel	chisels	chiseled chiselled	chiseling chiselling
15.	damsel	damsels	tinsel	counselor counsellor
16.	morsel	morsels	tassel	tassels
17.	vessel	vessels	sequel	sequels
18.	marvel	marvels	**marvelous**	marvelously
19.	**jewel**	jewels	jeweler	jewelry
20.	**towel**	towels	trowel	trowels
21.	vowel	vowels	pretzels	mazel tov
22.	* **counsel**	counsels	counseled counselled	counseling counselling
23.	* **council**	councils	councilor councillor	councilors councillors
24.	**pencil**	pencils	pupil	pupils
25.	stencil	stencils	vigil	vigils

*Homophones:

counsel/council   The lawyer had to counsel the city council.

	109th day	110th day	111th day	112th day
1.	peril	perils	perilous	perilously
2.	imperil	imperils	imperiled imperilled	imperiling imperilling
3.	**April**	April's rains	tonsil	tonsils
4.	utensil	utensils	fossil	fossils
5.	**evil**	evils	boll weevil	weevils
6.	**devil**	devils	daffodil	daffodils
7.	bedevil	bedevils	bedeviled bedevilled	bedeviling bedevilling
8.	civil	uncivil	civilian	civilians
9.	civilize	civilized	civilization	civility
10.	Virgil	Brazil	jonquil	jonquils
11.	tranquil	tranquilize tranquilise	tranquilizer tranquiliser	tranquility
12.	**owl**	owls	jowl	jowls
13.	howl	howls	howled	howling
14.	scowl	scowls	scowled	scowling
15.	growl	growls	growled	growling
16.	prowl	prowls	prowled	prowling
17.	*fowl	fowls	prowler	prowlers
18.	*bowl	bowls	bowled	bowling
19.	bowler	bowlers	**sugar!** bowl	the Rose Bowl
20.	**fuel**	fuels	fueled fuelled	fueling fuelling
21.	refuel	refuels	refueled refuelled	refueling refuelling
22.	*duel	duels	dueled duelled	dueling duelling
23.	**cruel**	cruelly	cruelty	**salve!**
24.	gruel	grueling gruelling	**usual**	usually
25.	*dual	duals	unusual	unusually

*Homophones:

fowl/foul   What do you call a bad-tasting bird? A foul fowl.

bowl/boll   You can have a bowl of cereal or bowl a strike. A boll weevil destroys cotton crops.

duel/dual   What do you call two sets of twins fighting each other? A dual duel.

! Insane Words: sugar ("shuug gur") salve ("SAV").

	113th day	114th day	115th day	116th day
1.	bulb	tulip bulbs	bulb	light bulbs
2.	bald	balding	baldness	bald
3.	scald	scalds	scalded	scalding
4.	Donald	Donald's	McDonald	McDonald's
5.	Ronald	Ronald	MacDonald	MacDonald's
6.	**field**	fields	fielded	fielding
7.	fielder	fielders	infield	outfield
8.	infielder	infielders	outfielder	outfielders
9.	wield	wields	wielded	wielding
10.	yield	yields	yielded	yielding
11.	shield	shields	shielded	shielding
12.	windshield	windshields	builder	builders
13.	* **build**	builds	**built**	**building**
14.	gild**	gilds	gilt**	gilding
15.	guild**	guilds	**guilt****	**guilty**
16.	plebe	plebes	plebian	cubing
17.	**tube**	tubes	tubing	cubic
18.	cube	cube	cubes	cubical
19.	**probable**	probably	probability	probabilities
20.	indescribable	indescribably	manageable	unmanageable
21.	readable	unreadable	readability	abilities
22.	commendable	commendably	marriageable	knowledgeable
23.	dependable	dependably	dependability	changeable
24.	expendable	peaceable	peaceably	unchangeable
25.	replaceable	irreplaceable	agreeable	agreeably

* Homophones:

build/billed   We like to build bird houses. We don't like to be billed for bird houses.

**Heteronyms:

gild/guild   She wanted gild the picture frame. Members of the wedding guild help at weddings.
gilt/guilt   The frame was gilt-edged. I felt a pang of guilt.

	117th day	118th day	119th day	120th day
1.	traceable	untraceable	serviceable	likeable
2.	noticeable	noticeably	unenforceable	saleable
3.	sizeable	unspeakable	unreasonable	irreparable
4.	affable	unbreakable	unreasonably	irreparably
5.	indefatigable	unthinkable	unseasonably	innumerable
6.	navigable	remarkable	personable	venerable
7.	teachable	remarkably	capable	vulnerable
8.	unteachable	workable	capability	invulnerable
9.	untouchable	available	capabilities	operable
10.	laughable	unavailable	incapable	inoperable
11.	appreciable	syllable	inescapable	miserable
12.	appreciably	monosyllable	bearable	miserably
13.	sociable	**flammable**#	unbearable	admirable
14.	sociably	**inflammable**#	parable	admirably
15.	unsociable	attainable	parables	desirable
16.	unsociably	imaginable	separable	undesirable
17.	**society**	unimaginable	inseparable	adorable
18.	**social**	pardonable	** **separate** rooms	deplorable
19.	socially	unpardonable	separately	memorable
20.	anti-social	fashionable	comparable	honorable
21.	liable	fashionably late	comparably	honorably
22.	**reliable**	unfashionable	incomparable	favorable
23.	unreliable	companionable	considerable	favorably
24.	undeniable	impressionable	considerably	honourable
25.	undeniably	questionable	insufferable	favourable

** **Heteronyms:**

separate adj. ("SEP rit")/separate v. ("SEP uh RAY't")

Synonyms:

The words flammable and inflammable have the same meanings.

Evaluation Test #3 (After 120 Days)

		Pattern being tested	Lesson word is i
1.	Do you like standing in a rec**eiving** line?	ceiving	84
2.	Most people enjoy going to a wedding rec**eption**.	ception	84
3.	I like people who are ch**eerful**.	eerful	85
4.	They did what they were asked to do ch**eerfully**.	eerfully	86
5.	It's no fun losing your l**uggage** on vacation.	age	87
6.	Sometimes it's necessary to have a strict b**udget**.	udge	89
7.	When was post**age** less than a dime?	age	91
8.	Cattle are sl**aughtered** everyday in stockyards.	aughtered	91
9.	My neighbor enjoys lifting w**eights**.	eights	94
10.	The sq**ueaky** wheel gets the grease.	eaky	95
11.	Our motor needs to be overh**auled**.	auled	99
12.	The two reb**els** were caught and tried for treason.	els	98
13.	Not all reb**ellions** are successful.	ellions	99
14.	Some people are very imp**ulsive**.	ulsive	104
15.	I dislike people who are always qu**arreling** (quarrelling).	arreling	108
16.	People should act civ**ilized**.	ivilized	110
17.	The pr**owlers** were caught by the police.	owlers	112
18.	The outf**ielders** collided going for the flyball.	ielders	116
19.	They prob**ably** didn't hear each other yell, "It's mine."	obably	114
20.	The mayor was unav**ailable** for comment.	ailable	118

Both -eling and -elling are correct; but expect consistency. Either all words like quarrel, shovel, tunnel, etc. should take double -l's in the -ed and -ing forms or just single -l's. Single l's are the traditional American spelling; double l's, British.

	121st day	122nd day	123rd day	124th day
1.	variable	unquestionably	tolerable	incurable
2.	invariably	reasonable	intolerable	durable
3.	pleasurable	excitable	accountable	believable
4.	measurable	profitable	accountability	unbelievable
5.	immeasurable	profitably	unaccountable	forgivable
6.	advisable	profitability	notable	unforgivable
7.	advisability	unprofitable	notably	livable
8.	inadvisable	imitable	potable	unlivable
9.	indispensable	inimitable	potent potables	lovable
10.	disposable	hospitable	quotable	lovably
11.	passable	inhospitable	adaptable	unlovable
12.	passably	hospitality	adaptability	movable
13.	impassable	hospital	**acceptable**	immovable
14.	usable	charitable	unacceptable	allowable
15.	unusable	charitably	**comfortable**	taxable
16.	excusable	veritable	comfortably	payable
17.	inexcusable	veritably	uncomfortable	unpayable
18.	debatable	**irritable**	**portable**	employable
19.	**respectable**	irritability	detestable	unemployable
20.	respectability	suitable	regrettable	employability
21.	**predictable**	suitably	regrettably	recognizable
22.	predictability	unsuitable	irrefutable	unrecognizable
23.	unpredictable	inevitable	irrefutably	allowable
24.	predictably	inevitability	indisputable	observable
25.	**vegetables**	lamentable	inscrutable	unobservable

	125th day	126th day	127th day	128th day
1.	marketable	presentable	valuable	constable
2.	uninhabitable	unpresentable	invaluable	inconceivable
3.	**Bible**	Bibles	bauble	baubles
4.	noble	nobles	nobility	nobler
5.	feeble	feebler	feeblest	feeble-minded
6.	ruble	rubles	foible	foibles
7.	**double**	doubles	doubled	doubling
8.	**trouble**	troubles	troubled	troubling
9.	**possible**	possibly	possibility	possibilities
10.	**impossible**	impossibly	impossibility	**salmon**!
11.	audible	audibly	audience	auditorium
12.	inaudible	inaudibly	audition	auditory nerves
13.	invincible	invincibly	invincibility	**psalm**!
14.	legible	legibly	legislature	legible
15.	illegible	illegibly	legislation	illegible
16.	forcible	forcibly	legislator	alleged
17.	enforceable	unenforceable	**legal**	allegiance
18.	edible	reducible	**illegal**	sieve
19.	inedible	irreducible	legality	legalities
20.	credible	credibly	credibility	**niece**
21.	incredible	incredibly	sieve	**nephew**
22.	intelligible	intelligibly	intelligent	intelligence
23.	incorrigible	incorrigibly	incorrigibility	incorrigibles
24.	tangible	tangibles	tangibly	tangibility
25.	intangible	intangibles	intangibly	intangibility

! Insane words:

salmon ("SAM mun") has a silent l.

psalm ("SAH'm") has a silent p and a silent l.

	129th day	130th day	131st day	132nd day
1.	indelible	indelibly	neglect	**psalm**
2.	negligible	negligibly	negligent	negligence
3.	fallible	fallibly	fallacy	fallacies
4.	infallible	infallibly	infallibility	fallacious
5.	gullible	gullibly	gullibility	**debts**
6.	discernible	discernibly	discernibility	indebted
7.	indiscernible	indiscernibly	**It's** mediocre.	**They're** mediocre.
8.	**terrible**	terribly	**terror**	terrified
9.	**horrible**	horribly	horror	horrified
10.	feasible	feasibly	feasibility	**There's** no hope.
11.	infeasible	infeasibly	infeasibility	**You're** right.
12.	visible	visibly	visibility	vision
13.	invisible	invisibly	invisibility	visionary
14.	divisible	divisibly	division	divide
15.	indivisible	indivisibly	**They're** nice people.	**We're** going **too.**
16.	defensible	defensibly	defense defence**	defensive defencive**
17.	indefensible	indefensibly	**They're** in **debt.**	**We're** in **debt too.**
18.	reprehensible	reprehensibly	comprehension	comprehensive
19.	comprehensible	comprehensibly	comprehensibility	comprehend
20.	apprehensible	incomprehensibly	apprehend	apprehension
21.	**sensible**	sensibly	sensibility	sensibilities
22.	**responsible**	responsibly	responsibility	responsibilities
23.	irresponsible	irresponsibly	responsive	irresponsible
24.	reversible	reversibly	mediocre	**mustache**!
25.	irreversible	irreversibly	mediocrity	deuce

** Homophones:

defense (American spelling) / defence (British spelling)

! Insane Words: mustache ("MUSS tash")

	133rd day	134th day	135th day	136th day
1.	impassible	impassibly	deuce	deuces
2.	**possible**	**possibly**	**possibility**	**possibilities**
3.	**impossible**	impossibly	impossibility	**mustache**!
4.	accessible	permit	permission	permissive
5.	inaccessible	inaccessibly	inaccessibility	**They're** going, **too.**
6.	irrepressible	irrepressibly	irrepressibility	**It's** too bad.
7.	admissible	inadmissible	admissibility	inadmissibility
8.	permissible	impermissible	permissibility	**We're** going to go.
9.	plausible	implausible	plausibility	implausible
10.	compatible	incompatible	compatibility	incompatibility
11.	destructible	indestructible	indestructibility	indestructible
12.	perceptible	imperceptible	contemptible	susceptible
13.	convertible	convertibles	suggestible	suggestibility
14.	digestible	indigestible	resistible	irresistible
15.	exhaustible	inexhaustible	combustible	combustibles
16.	flexible	inflexible	flexibility	inflexible
17.	babble	babbles	babbled	babbling
18.	babbler	babblers	feud	feuding
19.	rabble	pebble	pebbles	pebbly
20.	scrabble	dribbler	dribblers	There's too many there.
21.	dribble	dribbles	dribbled	dribbling
22.	nibble	nibbles	nibbled	nibbling
23.	quibble	quibbles	quibbled	quibbling
24.	scribble	scribbles	scribbled	scribbling
25.	scribbler	scribblers	double	trouble

! Insane Words: mustache ("MUSS tash")

	137th day	138th day	139th day	140th day
1.	gobble	gobbles	gobbled	gobbling
2.	hobble	hobbles	hobbled	hobbling
3.	bobble	bobbles	bobbled	bobbling
4.	cobble	cobbles	cobbled	cobbling
5.	cobbler	cobblers	cobblestone	cobblestones
6.	**bubble**	bubbles	bubbled	bubbling
7.	**double**	doubles	doubled	doubling
8.	**trouble**	troubles	troubled	troubling
9.	stubble	rubble	feuds	feuded
10.	ladle	ladles	ladled	ladling
11.	cradle	cradles	cradled	cradling
12.	needle	needles	needled	needling
13.	tweedle	wheedle	wheedles	wheedling
14.	* idle	idles	idled	idling
15.	idly	idler	idol	idolize
16.	bridle	bridles	unbridled	bridal
17.	sidle	sidles	sidled	sidling
18.	boodle	boodles	noodle	noodles
19.	doodle	doodles	doodled	doodling
20.	poodle	poodles	doodler	doodlers
21.	dawdle	dawdles	dawdled	dawdling
22.	pilfer	pilfers	pilfered	pilfering
23.	**golf**	golfs	golfed	golfing
24.	golfer	golfers	wolves	werewolves
25.	wolf	wolfed down	wolfs down	wolfing

* Homophones:

idle/idol   What do you call a lazy god? An idle idol.

bridle/bridal   Horses canter down a bridle path. Brides walk down a bridal path.

	141st day	142nd day	143rd day	144th day
1.	gulf	gulfs	Gulf of Mexico	Persian Gulf
2.	engulf	engulfs	engulfed	engulfing
3.	bulge	bulges	bulged	bulging
4.	indulge	indulges	indulged	indulging
5.	divulge	divulges	divulged	divulging
6.	* **caulk**	caulks	caulked	caulking
7.	* **calk**	calks	calked	calking
8.	elk	elks	whelk	whelks
9.	folk	folks	folklore	folksy
10.	* **yolk**	yolks	polka	polkas
11.	* **yoke**	yokes	yoked	yoking
12.	bulk	bulky	bulkier	bulkiest
13.	sulk	sulks	sulked	sulking
14.	skulk	skulks	skulked	skulking
15.	hulk	hulks	feuds	feuded
16.	elm	elms	helm	helms
17.	whelm	whelms	helmet	helmets
18.	underwhelm	underwhelms	spaghetti	spaghetti
19.	overwhelm	overwhelms	overwhelmed	overwhelming
20.	film	films	filmed	filming
21.	gulp	gulps	gulped	gulping
22.	pulp	pulps	pulpy	pulpit
23.	* **false**	falsely	false alarm	false alarms
24.	falsehood	falsehoods	false face	false faces
25.	falsify	falsifies	falsified	falsifying

* Homophones:

false/faults	What do you call untrue imperfections? False faults.
caulk/calk	You can caulk a crack or calk a crack, your choice.
yolk/yoke	The center (yellow part) of an egg is the yolk. You can yoke oxen to a plow.

	145th day	146th day	147th day	148th day
1.	or **else**	elsewhere	elsewise	or else
2.	**pulse**	pulses	choir	convulsive
3.	impulse	impulses	impulsive	impulsively
4.	repulse	repulses	repulsive	convulsion
5.	convulse	convulses	convulsed	convulsing
6.	**salt**	salts	salted	salting
7.	**salty**	saltier	saltiest	Malta
8.	malt	malts	malted milk	malteds
9.	**halt**	halts	halted	halting
10.	exalt	exalts	exalted	exalting
11.	**fault**	* **faults**	faulted	faulting
12.	faulty	faultier	faultiest	**choirs**
13.	default	defaults	defaulted	defaulting
14.	vault	vaults	vaulted	vaulting
15.	pole vaulter	pole vaulters	pole vaulter	pole vaulters
16.	pole vault	pole vaults	pole vaulted	pole vaulting
17.	**assault**	assaults	assaulted	assaulting
18.	somersault	somersaults	somersaulted	somersaulting
19.	* **Sault Ste. Marie**	spelt#	shelter	shelters
20.	**belt**	belts	belted	belting
21.	**melt**	melts	melted	melting
22.	smelt	smelts	smelted	smelting
23.	pelt	pelts	pelted	pelting
24.	welt	welts	welter	sweltered
25.	**dealt**!	swelter	swelters	sweltering

* **Homophones:**

Sault/Sioux/sue/Soo   People from the Soo (Sault Ste. Marie) have heard of Sioux City Sue.

Sault Ste. Marie ("SOO SAY'n-t muh REE") Usuallly the abbreviation for the title Saint is St., but since these U.S. and Canadian cities were named by the early French explorers, the feminine French abbreviation for Saint (Ste.) is used. In French, the masculine is St. the feminine, Ste. In Spanish the feminine is Santa (Santa Rosa) and the masculine is San (San Francisco).

! Note: dealt ("delt") In many "eel" words such as *feel*, the past tense is "elt." The past tense of *deal* ("deel") is *dealt* ("delt").

Note: In American English, the past tense (-ed form) of the word *spell* is *spelled*. However, in British English the older form (-elt) is used to form *spelt*. Compare feel/felt.

	149th day	150th day	151st day	152nd day
1.	**bolt**	bolts	bolted	bolting
2.	unbolt	unbolts	unbolted	unbolting
3.	thunderbolt	thunderbolts	colt	colts
4.	jolt	jolts	jolted	jolting
5.	**volt**	volts	revolution	revolutionary
6.	revolt	revolts	revolted	revolting
7.	**molt**	molts	molted	molting
8.	**moult****	moults	moulted	moulting
9.	**adult**	adults	**choir**	**choirs**
10.	**insult**	insults	insulted	insulting
11.	**result**	results	resulted	resulting
12.	consult	consults	consulted	consultation
13.	exult	exults	exulted	exultation
14.	catapult	catapults	catapulted	catapulting
15.	cult	cults	occult	spaghetti
16.	**difficult**	difficulty	difficulties	difficult
17.	waltz	waltzes	waltzed	waltzing
18.	**silver**	silvery	Silver's hoofs	silver
19.	**solve**	solves	solved	solution
20.	dissolve	dissolves	dissolved	dissolution
21.	revolve	revolves	revolved	revolution
22.	absolve	absolves	absolved	absolution
23.	involve	involves	involved	involution
24.	resolve	resolves	resolved	resolution
25.	**salve**!	salves	calves	halves

*Homophones:

molt/moult   Either spelling is correct.

! Insane words:

salve ("SAV")Rhymes with have. The letter l is silent.

	153rd day	154th day	155th day	156th day
1.	**aim**	aims	aimed	aiming
2.	**claim**	claims	claimed	claiming
3.	reclaim	reclaims	reclaimed	** reclamation
4.	acclaim	acclaims	acclaimed	** acclamation
5.	**exclaim**	exclaims	exclaimed	** exclamation
6.	proclaim	proclaims	proclaiming	** proclamation
7.	disclaim	disclaims	disclaimer	disclaimers
8.	maim	maims	maimed	maiming
9.	madam	madams	William	William's
10.	macadam	Gotham City	bedlam	balsam
11.	Islam	Islamic	wigwam	wigwams
12.	**program**	programs	**They're** winning.	**Their** dog died.
13.	* **programme**	** programmes	programmed	programming
14.	anthem	anthems	mayhem	**You're** okay.
15.	emblem	emblems	**It's too** late.	**Your** hat fell off.
16.	**problem**	problems	problematic	problematical
17.	**item**	items	itemize	itemization
18.	totem	totems	**We're** going.	**They're** losing.
19.	**system**	systems	systematic	systematically
20.	solemn	solemnly	solemnity	**Your** cat hurt its paw.
21.	**victim**	victims	victimize	**You're** right!
22.	pilgrim	pilgrims	pilgrimage	pilgrimages
23.	denim	blue denims	**You're** all right.	**Your** right hand.
24.	*** seraphim	*** cherubim	*** goyim	**They're** coming.
25.	verbatim	**They're** all right.	**Their** dog died.	**We're** almost **there.**

* **Homophones:**

program/programme   Americans prefer to program computers. The British programme them.

** **Vowel & Accent shift**

The long a sound (spelled ai) in the base *claim* changes to the schwa ("uh") sound spelled by the letter a when adding -ation ("AY shun").

*** **Irregular Plural**

Occasionally we keep the plural endings of words we borrow from other languages. For example, in Latin words ending in –us have the plural i as in one alumnus and many alumni. In these cases, the plural form is from the Hebrew language. One seraph, one cherub, one goy. Many seraphim, cherubim, and goyim.

	157th day	158th day	159th day	160th day
1.	**animal**	animals	animate	animation
2.	decimal	decimals	decimate	decimated
3.	mammal	mammals	**They're** our friends.	**There** are lots of reasons.
4.	thermal	thermometer	thermometers	They want **their** money.
5.	**formal**	formals	formally	formality
6.	informal	**Their** car is gone.	informally	informality
7.	**normal**	abnormal	normally	abnormality
8.	dismal	dismally	baptismal records	**They're** losing.
9.	to whom?	by whom?	for whom?	against whom?
10.	freedom	freedoms	random	randomly
11.	boredom	seldom	Christendom	martyrdom
12.	**wise**	fathom	fathoms	snake venom
13.	wisdom	idiom	idioms	idiomatic
14.	axiom	axioms	axiomatic	**We're** winning.
15.	pogrom	pogroms	phantom	phantoms
16.	ransom	ransoms	ransomed	ransoming
17.	blossom	blossoms	blossomed	blossoming
18.	**atom**	atoms	atomic	** **aluminum**
19.	**symptom**	symptoms	symptomatic	** **aluminium**
20.	**custom**	customs	customize	customer
21.	**bottom**	bottoms	bottomed	bottoming
22.	museum	museums	calcium	gymnasium
23.	radium	helium	**premium**	premiums
24.	**stadium**	stadiums	uranium	**auditorium**
25.	**medium**	tedium	geranium	geraniums

** Note: *aluminum/aluminium*

Americans use the spelling aluminum ("uh LOO min um"); the British use aluminium ("AL yoo MIN ee um").

Evaluation Test #4 (After 160 Days)

		Pattern being tested	Lesson word is in
1.	I just love Southern hospit**ality**.	ality	122
2.	I wish you would stop being so irrit**able**.	able	122
3.	Your handwriting is absolutely illeg**ible**.	ible	125
4.	Your work is incred**ibly** good.	ibly	126
5.	We all have different responsib**ilities**.	ilities	132
6.	There ought to be room in the program for flex**ibility.**	ility	135
7.	Just what is tr**oubling** you?	oubling	140
8.	I wish you would stop n**eedling** me.	eedling	140
9.	That movie was just absolutely overwh**elming**.	elming	144
10.	I would love to hear a rapper sing a f**olk** song.	olk	141
11.	Everyone should have a good strong p**ulse**.	ulse	145
12.	There's no excuse for **ass****aulting** another person.	aulting	148
13.	What a rev**olting** development this is.	olting	152
14.	Have you ever kept a New Year's res**olution**?	olution	152
15.	What's the pr**oblem**?	oblem	153
16.	All syst**ems** are go.	tems	154
17.	The governor procl**aimed** today as NOW day.	aimed	155
18.	That was an official procl**amation**.	amation	156
19.	Do you know the sym**ptoms** of pellagra?	ptoms	158
20.	They held the school play in the audit**orium**.	orium	160

	161st day	162nd day	163rd day	164th day
1.	potassium	planetarium	solarium	barium
2.	titanium	Belgium	aquarium	delirium
3.	magnesium	symposium	emporium	sanitarium
4.	amber	ambergris	somber	somberly
5.	ember	embers	September	September's child
6.	**member**	members	November	November's child
7.	**remember**	**remembers**	**remembered**	remembering
8.	dismember	dismembers	dismembered	dismembering
9.	limber	limbers	limbered	limbering
10.	timber	timbers	timbered	timbering
11.	lumber	lumbers	lumbered	lumbering
12.	slumber	slumbers	slumbered	slumbering
13.	**number**	numbers	numbered	numbering
14.	misnumber	misnumbers	misnumbered	misnumbering
15.	encumber	encumbers	encumbered	encumbering
16.	**cucumber**	cucumbers	chamber	chambers
17.	amble	ambles	ambled	ambling
18.	ramble	rambles	rambled	rambling
19.	gamble	gambles	gambled	gambling
20.	gambler	gamblers	rambler	ramblers
21.	scramble	scrambles	scrambled eggs	scrambling
22.	scrambler	scramblers	shambles	nimble
23.	tremble	trembles	trembled	trembling
24.	assemble	assembled	**assembly**	assemblies
25.	disassemble	disassembles	disassembled	disassembling

53

	165th day	166th day	167th day	168th day
1.	resemble	resembles	resembling	resemblance
2.	thimble	thimbles	Wimbledon	nimbly
3.	humble	humbles	humbled	humbling
4.	**tumble**	tumbles	tumbled	tumbling
5.	**stumble**	stumbles	stumbled	stumbling
6.	jumble	jumbles	jumbled	jumbling
7.	**fumble**	fumbles	fumbled	fumbling
8.	**mumble**	mumbles	mumbled	mumbling
9.	rumble	rumbles	rumbled	rumbling
10.	**grumble**	grumbles	grumbled	grumbling
11.	**theme**	themes	**supreme**	supremely
12.	scheme	schemes	schemed	scheming
13.	**extreme**	extremes	extremity	extremities
14.	**extremely**	unassuming	assumption	assumptions
15.	**assume**	assumes	assumed	assuming
16.	costume	costumes	costumed	costuming
17.	consume	consumes	consumed	consuming
18.	consumer	consumers	consumption	presumption
19.	presume	presumes	presumed	presuming
20.	** **resume**	resumes	resumed	resuming
21.	plume	plumes	resumption	gumption
22.	fume	fumes	fumed	fuming
23.	**perfume**	perfumes	ghetto	ghettos
24.	**empty**	empties	emptied	emptying
25.	Humpty	Humpty Dumpty	H. Dumpty's fall	spaghetti

** Heteronyms:

resume/resumé To begin again is to resume ("ree ZOOM").

To make a list of all your jobs and positions is to write your resumé ("REZ zuh MAY").

Sequential Spelling Level 4 - Teacher's Guide

	169th day	170th day	171st day	172nd day
1.	hemp	Kemp	temp	choirboy
2.	**temper**	tempers	tempered	tempering
3.	temperature	temperatures	distemper	chorus
4.	tamper	tampers	tampered	tampering
5.	**camper**	campers	damper	dampers
6.	pamper	**pampers**	**pampered**	pampering
7.	whimper	whimpers	whimpered	whimpering
8.	simper	simpers	simpered	simpering
9.	romper	rompers	**bumper**	bumpers
10.	**jumper**	jumpers	plumper	Thumper
11.	ample	amply	example	examples
12.	**sample**	samples	sampled	sampling
13.	trample	tramples	trampled	trampling
14.	**temple**	temples	sampler	samplers
15.	**simple**	simpler	simplest	simply
16.	**pimple**	pimples	pimpled	pimply
17.	**dimple**	dimples	dimpled	dimpling
18.	rumple	rumples	rumpled	rumpling
19.	**crumple**	crumples	crumpled	crumpling
20.	**again**	again and again	against	up against it
21.	**mountain**	mountains	mountainous	conquer
22.	**fountain**	fountains	uncertain	unconquered
23.	**certain**	certainly	certainty	uncertainty
24.	villain	villains	villainous	villainously
25.	**bargain**	bargains	bargained	bargaining

	173rd day	174th day	175th day	176th day
1.	**captain**	captains	captained	captaining
2.	**curtain**	curtains	Britain	Britain's economy
3.	urban	suburban	interurban	Dominican
4.	turban	turbans	Michael Jordan	conqueror
5.	Mohican	Mohicans	pagan	pagans
6.	publican	publicans	slogan	slogans
7.	**Republican**	Republicans	toboggan	toboggans
8.	pelican	pelicans	cardigan	cardigans
9.	Anglican	Anglicans	organ	organs
10.	**American**	Americans	Gilligan	Gilligan's Island
11.	**African**	Africans	Jonathan	Jonathan's
12.	**Mexican**	Mexicans	veteran	veterans
13.	**Canadian**	Canadians	Texan	Texans
14.	**ocean**	oceans	Atlantic Ocean	Pacific Ocean
15.	Arab	Arabia	Arabian	Arabic
16.	***Colombia**	Colombian	library	librarian
17.	***Columbia**	Italy	Italian	Italians
18.	median	medians	vegetarian	vegetarians
19.	comedian	comedians	history	historian
20.	**Indian**	Indians	Indiana	Indiana's Indians
21.	**Australian**	Australians	college	collegian
22.	veterinarian	veterinarians	ruffian	ruffians
23.	Mongol	Mongolia	Mongolian	Mongolians
24.	**Christ**	**Christmas**	**Christian**	**Christianity**
25.	Norway	Norwegian	theology	theologian

*Homophones:

Colombia/Columbia   Washington, D.C. is the District of Columbia. We get a lot of coffee from Colombia.

	177th day	**178th day**	**179th day**	**180th day**
1.	**magic**	**magician**	magicians	magically
2.	logic	logician	logicians	logically
3.	Phoenicia	Phoenician	Phoenicians	**They're too** much.
4.	technical	technician	technicians	technically
5.	**electric**	**electrician**	electricians	electrically
6.	obstetrics	obstetrician	obstetricians	**You're** going **too**?
7.	**music**	**musician**	musicians	musically
8.	physic	**physician**	physicians	physically
9.	arithmetic	arithmetician	arithmeticians	arithmetically
10.	**politics**	**politician**	politicians	politically
11.	optic	optician	opticians	optically
12.	statistic	statistician	statisticians	statistically
13.	Confucius	Confucian	Confucians	**We're** not feuding.
14.	**Asia**	**Asian**	Asians	Asiatic
15.	Caucasus	Caucasian	Caucasians	chorus
16.	Eurasia	Eurasian	Eurasians	* chords
17.	Paris	Parisian	Parisians	**Their** cat chased our dog.
18.	Persia	Persian	Persians	**It's** almost time.
19.	Russia	Russian	Russians	**That's too** bad.
20.	Prussia	Prussian	Prussians	old-fashioned
21.	issue#	issues	issued	issuing
22.	tissue#	tissues	cushion	cushions
23.	fashion	fashions	fashioned	fashioning
24.	**Jose**** Gonzales	**Jesus**** Gonzales	**Jose** Gonzales	**Jesus** Gonzales
25.	**frijoles****	frijoles	frijoles	frijoles

* **Homophones:**

chords/cords   Musicians play with chords. Woodsmen work with cords of wood.

** **"FANCY" Words:**

Jose / Jesus / frijoles   In Spanish, the letter J is pronounced as an H, so Jose is pronounced "HO ZAY" and Jesus is pronounced "HAY ZOO-ss" and frijoles is pronounced "free HO layz."

Note: issue / tissue   In these words the letters ss have the sound of /sh/.

Final Evaluation Test

	Sentence	Pattern being tested	Lesson word is in
1.	We have some unfin**ished** business to attend to.	ished	4
2.	Actors just love appl**ause**.	ause	20
3.	Famili**arity** breeds contempt.	arity	18
4.	My older sister is an electri**cian**.	cian	24
5.	AVKO spe**cial**izes in helping people learn.	cial	34
6.	Do you like previews of coming attr**actions**?	actions	48
7.	How many of the psychic's pre**dictions** came true?	dictions	60
8.	How do you think I arrived at that concl**usion**?	usion	68
9.	We gave them new sw**eaters** for their anniversary.	eaters	80
10.	My sister works for a constr**uction** company.	uction	64
11.	Do you like standing in a re**ceiving** line?	ceiving	84
12.	Most people enjoy going to a wedding re**ception**.	ception	84
13.	Cattle are sl**aughtered** everyday in stockyards.	aughtered	91
14.	Some people are very imp**ulsive**.	ulsive	104
15.	The mayor was un**available** for comment.	ailable	118
16.	I just love Southern hospit**ality**.	ality	122
17.	We all have different respons**ibilities**.	ilities	132
18.	Have you ever kept a New Year's resol**ution**?	olution	152
19.	The governor procl**aimed** today as NOW day.	aimed	155
20.	That was an official procl**amation**.	amation	156
21.	Have you re**membered** everything I've taught you?	membered	163
22.	Never eat scr**ambled** eggs that have turned green.	ambled	163
23.	Be careful when making an ass**umption** about anything.	umption	167
24.	I hate to hear a dog wh**impering**.	impering	172
25.	I have a friend who has become a veget**arian**.	arian	175

Answer Key

Day 1
Fill in the blank with words from today's spelling list.
1. In some denominations, there is a **parish** council.
2. It was **foolish** of you to think your dad wouldn't notice the dent in the car.
3. How much work do you have left to **finish**? I want to go to the mall.
4. What did you **accomplish** today?
5. My friend Paula is half **Polish**. Her father immigrated last year.
6. Did anyone **perish** in the fire last night?
7. Don't you think you're being a little **selfish**?
8. My mom teaches **English** at the high school.
9. Alicia's feet are very **ticklish**.
10. Jon broke his ankle in two places in a very **freakish** bike accident.

Day 3
Unscramble these:
1. eprehlisab — perishable
2. nihsdelutnossa — outlandishness
3. lseispoh — polishes
4. hrlsi — Irish
5. wehiJs — Jewish
6. vledtriy — deviltry
7. esolsdr — solders
8. getuon — tongue
9. epdioccmhals — accomplished
10. elsehidr — relished

Day 4
Can You Find the Words?

```
S + + + + + + + H + + G + S +
+ T + + + S + + + S N + P + H
+ + N + + + O + + I I A + S +
+ + + E + + + L H + N N I + +
+ + D + M + + S D I + N N + +
+ + E + + H I + S E A + + I +
S + H + + L S H + D R + + R F
E + S + O + + I + + + E + U +
U + I P + + + + L + + + D B +
G + N + + + + + + P + + + B +
N + I + + + + + + + M + + I +
O + F S T U D E N T S O + S +
T + N + + T H E I R + + C H +
+ + U + + + + + + + + + + C +
+ + + + + + + H S I T I R B A
```

(Over, Down, Direction)
ACCOMPLISHMENTS(15,15,NW)
BRITISH(14,15,W)
DANISH(10,7,NE)
FINNISH(15,7,NW)
POLISHING(4,9,NE)
RUBBISH(14,7,S)
SOLDERED(6,2,SE)
SPANISH(14,1,SW)
STUDENTS(4,12,E)
THEIR(6,13,E)
TONGUES(1,13,N)
UNFINISHED(3,14,N)

Day 5
Fill in the blank with words from today's spelling list.
1. Chicken soup can **nourish** the body.
2. No one can make a plate of homemade chocolate chip cookies **vanish** faster than Steve.
3. In the middle ages, torture was a very common way to **punish** people.
4. Hosta is a plant that will **flourish** in the shade.
5. Lawyers need to **establish** the facts of a legal case.
6. After graduation, the six of us are going to Jack's **cabin** for the weekend.
7. I always look forward to seeing a **robin**, it means spring is here!
8. At my grandfather's funeral, the **coffin** was draped with an American flag.

Day 6
Unscramble these:
1. erdimkhsis — skirmished
2. hpnudsie — punished
3. sgohunrnii — nourishing
4. baetsedshil — established
5. hienddsmii — diminished
6. hotisnsade — astonished
7. fiafparn — paraffin
8. gnfamuarif — ragamuffin
9. bicenat — cabinet
10. lsdemiblehe — embellished

Day 11
Fill in the blanks with words from today's spelling list.
1. Nathan ate dinner at **their** house.
2. Paul, **your** friend left a message for you.
3. **We're** on our way to the movies.
4. Carter said **they're** coming over tonight.
5. Because of the rain, there **were** delays at the airport.
6. I think **you're** the best friend ever!
7. **There** is an exciting movie playing at the theatre this weeked.
8. Did you finish **your** chores yet?
9. You can have another cookie if **there** is one left.
10. **You're** always late!

Day 12

```
+ N T O X I N S P + N + Y A Y
H + O + + + + E + I + L S + L
+ A + I + + N + L + D S S + L
+ + I + T G + L + I A + E + A
+ + + R U A I + L S + + U + N
+ + + I P C C O S + + + G + I
+ + N + I I S I + + + N S G
+ S + N + + N + X + + + O O R
+ + E + + A + S + O + + T L A
+ P + + T + + + + + T + + D M
+ + + I S O L D E R I N G I +
+ + O D E S O P P U S + I E +
G N I T A N I S S A S S A R +
S + + + + + + + + + + + + S +
+ + + + + + + + + + + + + + +
```

(Over,Down,Direction)
ASSASSINATING(13,13,W)
ASSASSINATIONS(14,1,SW)
HAIRPINS(1,2,SE)
INTOXICATION(13,12,NW)
MARGINALLY(15,10,N)
PENGUINS(9,1,SW)
PENICILLIN(2,10,NE)
SOLDERING(5,11,E)
SOLDIERS(14,7,S)
SOLIDLY(7,7,NE)
SUPPOSED(11,12,W)
TONGUES(13,9,N)
TOXINS(3,1,E)

Day 14
Choose the correct word for each sentence.
1. **I'll** be coming to your party.
2. The book is on the floor in the **aisle**.
3. This **isle** is a dream come true.
4. She looked beautiful walking down the **aisle** at the wedding.
5. **I'll** make the dip if you buy the chips.
6. Mark said the **isle** was deserted.
7. **Aisle** 7 needs to be cleaned.
8. It was a tropical **isle**.
9. It's such a pretty **aisle** with flowers on the benches.
10. **I'll** walk you to your car.

Day 15
Unscramble these:
1. iglfgledn — fledgling
2. inalds — island
3. esil — isle
4. iseal — aisle
5. noihngt — nothing
6. ndklcgiu — duckling
7. itwrne — winter
8. ntiryw — wintry
9. raprnetyc — carpentry
10. erptstay — tapestry

Day 19
Fill in the blanks with words from today's spelling list.
1. The cliffs were almost **perpendicular** to the sea.
2. Who is the most **popular** entertainer of your generation?
3. What a **peculiar** looking hat!
4. This **particular** sound went on and on.
5. The audience stood and **applauded** loudly when she finished her solo.
6. What a **spectacular** sunset!
7. She's a **regular** customer.
8. Even though Jack is very fit and **muscular**, he hurt his back while digging in the yard.

Day 20

```
+ + M + Y + + + + Y + C S S +
+ + + U + T + + T + I + P O +
Y + + S + I I + R + + I L +
+ L + + + C R R C + + H D +
+ + R + M A L U A + + + S E +
+ + + A L A L E + L + + R R +
R E G U L A R I T Y O + A I +
+ + P M R U + A + + + P L N +
+ O + O + + C + U + + S O G +
P + + L + + + I + D E + H N +
E S U A L P P A T L I + C I +
+ + + R + + + + B R + N S B +
+ + + + + + + U + + A + G U +
+ + + + + + A + + + + P + A +
+ + + + + B C I R C L E + D +
```

(Over,Down,Direction)
APPLAUSE(8,11,W)
BAUBLES(6,15,NE)
CIRCLE(7,15,E)
CIRCULAR(12,1,SW)
DAUBING(14,15,N)
MARAUDING(5,5,SE)
MOLAR(4,8,S)
MUSCLE(3,1,SE)
PARTICULARLY(12,14,NW)
POLARITY(12,8,NW)
POPULARITY(1,10,NE)
REGULARITY(1,7,E)
SCHOLARSHIPS(13,12,N)
SOLDERING(14,1,S)

Day 21
Sound alike words: (alter/altar; symbol/cymbal)
Circle the appropriate word to complete each sentence.
1. Please kneel at the (alter, altar). **altar**
2. A distaff is a (cymbal, symbol) of the home. **symbol**
3. We will need to (alter, altar) our travel arrangements. **alter**
4. My little brother cries when he hears a (cymbal, symbol) crash. **cymbal**
5. The robber tried to (alter, altar) his appearance. **alter**
6. A heart is the (cymbal, symbol) for love. **symbol**
7. The bride and groom held hands as they approached the (alter, altar). **altar**
8. Can you play a finger (cymbal, symbol)? **cymbal**

Day 22
Unscramble these:
1. enmceiid — medicine
2. sngiel — single
3. raugnsli — singular
4. gneal — angle
5. agnlaru — angular
6. heodmt — method
7. cfrfiat — traffic
8. opsdire — periods
9. ciamg — magic
10. eiretlcc — electric

Day 25
Fill in the blanks with words from today's spelling list.
1. In the summer, we like to take a **picnic** lunch to the beach.
2. Lisa called me in a **panic** because she couldn't find her car keys.
3. Jack attempted to **mimic** Steve's football moves with little success.
4. I spent most of the afternoon at the **clinic** waiting to see the doctor.
5. Jon's **mechanic** told him that the used car would need lots of repairs so he decided not to buy it.
6. We're going to spend our summer vacation near the **ocean** this year.
7. The paramedics arrived on the **scene** minutes after the car crash.
8. Ulysses was a **hero** of the Trojan Wars.
9. My mom bought me some beautiful batik **fabric** while she was in Bali.
10. Before going camping, we stocked up on the **basic** necessities, bread, peanut butter and jelly.

Day 27
Unscramble these:
1. eidpcicnk — picnicked
2. sphcsyi — physics
3. ibsettscro — obstetrics
4. ceakdpni — panicked
5. myceocloinal — economically
6. mcdkeimi — mimicked
7. ardma — drama
8. ftnacia — fanatic
9. laafctani — fanatical
10. tricdmaa — dramatic

Day 28

```
D I A B E T E S + + + + + A E
P R + + + + C + + + + F + N Z
A + A + + + O + + + A + + T I
N + + M + + N + + N + + G A G
I + + + A + O + A + L + N R O
C + + + + T M T + + Y + I C L
K Y L L A C I T N A R F K T O
I + + + + C Z C + + + I + C P
N + + + A + I + A + C + I C A
G + + + L + + N + + L A + N A +
+ + L + + + G + + + + L + C +
+ Y L L A C I M O C + Y I + +
+ + + M I M I C K I N G P + +
+ + + + N A I C I S Y H P + +
D I P L O M A T I C + + + + +
```

(Over, Down, Direction)
ANTARCTICA(14,1,S)   FANATICALLY(12,2,SW)
APOLOGIZE(15,9,N)   FRANTICALLY(12,7,W)
COMICALLY(10,12,W)   LYRICAL(11,5,S)
DIABETES(1,1,E)   MIMICKING(4,13,E)
DIPLOMATIC(1,15,E)   PANICKING(1,2,S)
DRAMATICALLY(1,1,SE)   PHYSICIAN(13,14,W)
ECONOMIZING(7,1,S)   PICNICKING(13,13,N)

Day 30
Unscramble these:
1. pcaeaulpe — applesauce
2. arkmepaece — peacemaker
3. suearscf — surfaces
4. srecvise — services
5. meiopssr — promises
6. ncrteipaeps — apprentices
7. eidpsurejc — prejudices
8. aeuplcef — peaceful
9. clsecaocmip — accomplices
10. senaemc — menaces

Day 31
Fill in the blanks using the correct word:
1. May I have another (piece, peace) of cake? **piece**
2. Mr. Smith was cited by the police for disturbing the (piece, peace). **peace**
3. Let's try to (piece, peace) this quilt before you leave. **piece**
4. The dove is the universal sign of (piece, peace). **peace**

Day 33
Complete the following sentences using they're, there or their.
1. They always take (they're, there, their) dog with them on vacation. **their**
2. Let's wait (they're, there, their) alongside the entrance to the mall. **there**
3. When you talk to them, ask if (they're, there, their) coming tomorrow. **they're**
4. (They're, There, Their) football team is going to the state championship game. **Their**
5. Dad was pleased that they had done so well on (they're, there, their) ACT tests. **their**
6. Her parents won't be joining us as (they're, there, their) both working that day. **they're**
7. Jack is always (they're, there, their) on time. **there**
8. (They're, There, Their) leaving for the airport at 12:30 today. **They're**

Day 35
Unscramble these:
1. narhco — anchor
2. chtsoam — stomach
3. ircaal — racial
4. lfiafoci — official
5. cjuiieldpar — prejudicial
6. uipisosusc — suspicious
7. iceylommrlac — commercially
8. oowpincelam — policewoman
9. rrocgey — grocery
10. sicedul — sluiced

Day 39
Unscramble these:
1. ckyheo — hockey
2. kcdroeedf — defrocked
3. dkcsohe — shocked
4. uedkcd — ducked
5. bdkuce — bucked
6. lyukc — lucky
7. edkncok — knocked
8. ekcbdlo — blocked
9. koccy — cocky
10. dlkaoecpd — padlocked

Day 40

```
G N I K C U L C + + S + G + +
+ + + + + + + T + T + N + +
+ + + + + + S + + O T I + +
+ + + + + E + B + C S K + +
D + + + + I + L + D K E + +
+ E + + K + O + E + I I O + +
R + R C + C + F + + N K M + +
+ O U O K + R + + + G C + + +
+ L C I H O G N I K C O L N U
+ + N K C C S N + + + C + + +
+ G + K I O N + I + + + + + +
+ + I + E E + A + K + + + + +
+ N + M + + S S H O C K I N G
G + A + + + + T + + + + O + +
+ C + + + + + + + + + R + +
```

(Over,Down,Direction)
ANCHORED(8,12,NW)   MOCKING(13,7,N)
BLOCKING(9,4,SW)   ROCKIEST(1,7,SE)
CAMEOS(2,15,NE)   ROCKING(13,15,NW)
CLUCKING(8,1,W)   SHOCKING(8,13,E)
COCKIEST(12,10,N)   STOCKING(11,1,S)
DEFROCKING(10,5,SW) UNLOCKING(15,9,W)
LUCKIEST(2,9,NE)

Day 41
Using Your Words:
Fill in the blank with words from your spelling list.
1. The accident report said that the **truck struck** the car first.
2. Do you know what a **particle** accelerator is?
3. Susan and Emily have the same **circle** of friends.
4. My **uncle** taught me how to ride a **bicycle** when I was five.
5. After we finishing digging out the shrubs in our yard, every **muscle** in my body ached.
6. The celebrations of the Millenium were quite a **spectacle**.
7. The second **act** of the play was the longest.

Day 47
Unscramble these:
1. rntcataito — attraction
2. ubntagtcris — subtracting
3. detrcancot — contracted
4. itccnonrtoa — contraction
5. itepdacm — impacted
6. caattrac — cataract
7. lrrcsaatlhaiyecti — charateristically
8. rdteaufcr — fractured
9. atcict — tactic
10. rtatorc — tractor

Day 49
Tricky Words: (affect/effect) Affect means to have an effect on or influence. Effect means result or fulfillment. Choose the correct word to complete each sentence.
1. This quiz will have no (affect, effect) on our final grade for the class. **effect**
2. I didn't expect that movie to (affect, effect) me the way it did. **affect**
3. Don't let those comments (affect, effect) you. affect
4. Allison likes the (affect, effect) of the color wash on her painting. **effect**
5. Skipping class regularly will have an (affect, effect) on your grades. **affect**
6. Our new rules are having the desired (affect, effect). **effect**
7. What (affect, effect) do you think the news will have? **effect**
8. No matter what the final decision is, it won't (affect, effect) me. **affect**

Day 52

```
+ + + N + + + A + S + N + +
P + Y + O + C F + N + O O + +
+ E + L + I F E O + I + I + +
+ + R + E E T I L T + + T Y +
+ + + F C V T C C L + + C L +
+ + + T E C I E E + O + E N +
+ + I + E C L T + J + + J V E
+ O + R + E T + C + E + B I G
N + I + S + + I + E + R O T L
+ D + + + + + + O J + + C E
N O I T C E F N I N + B + E C
E R E C T I N G + + + + O F T
+ + + + + + + + + + + + F I
E C N E G I L L E T N I + E N
+ + + + C O R R E C T I O N G
```

(Over,Down,Direction)
AFFECTION(9,1,SW)   INTELLIGENCE(12,14,W)
CELLO(7,2,SE)   NEGLECTING(15,6,S)
CORRECTION(5,15,E)   OBJECTION(13,9,N)
DIRECTIONS(2,10,NE) OBJECTIVELY(13,12,NW)
EFFECTIVELY(14,14,N) PERFECTION(1,2,SE)
ERECTING(1,12,E)   REJECTION(12,9,NW)
INFECTION(9,11,W)   SELECTION(5,9,NE)

Day 55
Unscramble these:
1. cxepdete — **expected**
2. unedpetxec — **unexpected**
3. isstcen — **insects**
4. tcutcraerehi — **architecture**
5. ileyeactllrc — **electrically**
6. uelcdetr — **lectured**
7. icusonspi — **suspicion**
8. iflgntueegcn — **genuflecting**
9. cnsusiiop — **suspicion**
10. spsetduce — **suspected**

Day 59
Unscramble these:
1. dtecidda — **addicted**
2. vyritoc — **victory**
3. ocioncnitartd — **contradiction**
4. ecbinienotd — **benediction**
5. soitcitnrre — **restriction**
6. decinttidre — **interdicted**
7. cntoodecc — **concocted**
8. drcoterpo — **proctored**
9. roocddte — **doctored**
10. gphticni — **pitching**

Day 63
Fill in the blank with words from today's spelling list.
1. The flight attendants **instructed** us to use the oxygen masks if the airplane's cabin lost pressure.
2. Are you more **productive** in the morning or afternoon?
3. Sam **doodled** on his paper while he waited for his dad to pick him up.
4. We watched as Mr. Smith **conducted** the science experiment.
5. While riding our bikes, we discovered that a house was being **constructed** on the vacant lot on Pine Street.
6. **Constructive** criticism is a good thing.
7. **Wouldn't** you rather have lemonade?
8. Do you think Susan **understood** that we wanted to meet her at noon?

Day 64

```
+ N + + + + + + + + + I + M N
+ N O I T C U R T S N O C I O
A + + I + + + + N S + G P S I
+ B + + T + + O T + + N R U T
+ + D + + C I R + + + I O N C
+ + + U + T U + + + + C D D U
+ + + + C C Y R + + + U U E D
+ + + U T T S L T + + D C R O
+ + D I + E I + N S + E E S R
+ E O + L + + O + E B D R T P
D N + D + + + N + D O S O + +
S C O N D U C T I N G O + O +
+ O S R E L D O O D + + O D +
P D O G W O O D + + + + + W +
+ + + + + + + + + + + + + + +
```

(Over,Down,Direction)
ABDUCTION(1,3,SE)   INSTRUCTIONS(12,1,SW)
CONDUCTING(2,12,E) MISUNDERSTOOD(14,1,S)
CONSTRUCTION(13,2,W) OBSTRUCTION(12,11,NW)
DEDUCING(12,10,N)   POODLES(1,14,NE)
DEDUCTIONS(1,11,NE) PRODUCERS(13,3,S)
DOGWOOD(2,14,E)   PRODUCTION(15,10,N)
DOODLERS(10,13,W)   WOODENLY(14,14,NW)

Day 66
Fill in the blanks with words from today's spelling list.
1. Another name for lie is **falsehood**.
2. What's the **likelihood** we'll have good weather for Aunt Stacy's wedding in November?
3. They built a **crude** shelter out of branches.
4. Both of us had bad **attitudes** today.
5. The spring **floods** were very serious this year.
6. We found that one of the **intruders** dropped his flashlight.
7. See how that rock **protrudes** from the side of the cliff?
8. I wrote a note to Lisa to thank her for **including** me in her birthday party.
9. Jack gave the **concluding** speech at graduation.
10. Do you ever get a **bloody** nose after you sneeze? I do.

Day 67
Tricky Words: (allude/elude)
Allude is a verb which means to refer indirectly
Elude is a verb which mean to escape or avoid
Complete the sentences with the correct word.

1. In his acceptance speech, Jack (alluded, eluded) to his high school drama teacher. **alluded**
2. The burglar (alluded, eluded) detection and escaped. **eluded**
3. The solution to this problem (alludes, eludes) me. **eludes**
4. Do you think the reference in the book (alludes, eludes) to his time in Spain? **alludes**
5. There was something I wanted to tell you, but it's (alluding, eluding) me at the moment. **eluding**
6. We didn't want to bring up the problem directly, but we tried to (allude, elude) to it so we could talk about it. **allude**

Day 68
Unscramble these:
1. dlfignoo — **flooding**
2. lonilsiu — **illusion**
3. lndiuseo — **delusion**
4. onuloisccn — **conclusion**
5. otheorhdom — **motherhood**
6. obenrohdosgih — **neighborhoods**
7. pdrmiay — **pyramid**
8. ldigeun — **eluding**
9. snllouia — **allusion**
10. cnslnouii — **inclusion**

Day 71
Unscramble these:
1. sutregian — **signature**
2. iadneogtsni — **designation**
3. nug — **gnu**
4. ieergrnosf — **foreigners**
5. ecldma — **calmed**
6. masnol — **salmon**
7. ottseonmb — **tombstone**
8. blam — **lamb**
9. brmoeb — **bomber**
10. iagtmnaln — **malignant**

Day 75
(**Whose/Who's**)
Choose the correct answer.
1. (Who's, Whose) going to choose the decorations for the part? **Who's**
2. (Who's, Whose) left foot is bigger? Yours or mine? **Whose**
3. I'm not sure sure (whose, who's) house we're going to first. **whose**
4. (Whose, Who's) the new student? **Who's**
5. Do you know (whose, who's) books are on the table? **whose**
6. I can't remember (whose, who's) bike I borrowed last week. **whose**
7. (Who's, Whose) running in the 10k this Saturday? **Who's**
8. (Who's, Whose) bringing the fruit for the smoothies we're making? **Who's**

Day 74
Unscramble these:
1. nwesrkli — wrinkles
2. twersslre — wrestlers
3. risrtew — writers
4. erhwtis — writhes
5. rwdoss — swords
6. terhwas — wreaths
7. hwftrula — wrathful
8. creneswh — wrenches
9. secrsae — creases
10. rsnwsae — answers

Day 76

```
+ + + S + + + + + R + + G + G
W + + W + + + + E + + N S + N
R + + O + + + L + + I T + + I
A + + R + G E + + G S + + + L
P W + D + A N + N I + + + + K
P + R F S G N I R E W S N A N
I + + I + + R W H + + + + + I
N + N G T W G + + C + + + G R
G G + H + H + N + + N + R + W
+ + + T G N I T I R W E + + Y
W R O N G S + N + S A + R + L
+ + + + + + + + G S A + + W L
D E C E A S E D I + + E + + O
+ + + + + + + N + + + + L + H
+ + + + + + G + + + + + + + W
```

(Over, Down, Direction)
ANSWERING(14,6,W)
DECEASED(1,13,E)
GREASING(14,8,SW)
LEASING(13,14,NW)
RELEASING(10,1,SW)
SWORDFIGHT(4,1,S)
WHOLLY(15,15,N)
WRAPPING(1,2,S)
WRENCHING(14,12,NW)
WRINGING(6,8,NE)
WRINKLING(15,9,N)
WRISTS(8,7,NE)
WRITHING(2,5,SE)
WRITING(11,10,W)
WRONGS(1,11,E)

Day 78
Unscramble these:
1. tghhwsievaye — heavyweights
2. byafolvar — favorably
3. rfaluosv — flavours
4. ecreisve — receives
5. esvale — leaves
6. rsabveee — bereaves
7. eevssel — sleeves
8. ervehia — heavier
9. vrelcsae — cleavers
10. aednfe — deafen

Day 79
Choose the correct answer.
1. According to legend, (they're, their, there) is buried treasure on the island. **there**
2. Gram and Gramps just called to tell us (they're, their, there) coming for a visit this week. **they're**
3. I can't wait to see the looks on (they're, their, there) faces when I bring Jack to the party! **their**
4. Do you know if (they're, their, there) planning to go to the movies with us? **they're**
5. I'm going to stay out of the discussion since it's (they're, their, there) decision. **their**
6. I think Emily left her glasses over (they're, their, there). **there**
7. They haven't called yet, I wonder if (they're, their, there) home yet. **they're**
8. (They're, Their, There) is a snake in my basket! **There**

Day 81
Fill in the blank with words from today's spelling list.
1. Did you **receive** the invitation to Allison's birthday party yet?
2. It's **inconceivable** that she wouldn't invite you!
3. Before the next snowstorm, we'll need to get a new **shovel**.
4. I felt just **dreadful** when I had pneumonia last week.
5. What's the most **shameful** thing you've done?
6. That was a very **forceful** argument in favor of extending your curfew!
7. The twins I babysit for are a **handful**.
8. The store clerk put the gift **receipt** in the box for me.

Day 82
Unscramble these:
1. ldesevhol — shovelled
2. pucealfe — peaceful
3. fluyee — eyeful
4. thouulfm — mouthful
5. eecropvecind — preconceived
6. ptceivere — receptive
7. vecedied — deceived
8. inilgec — ceiling
9. elhlsrvdie — shrivelled
10. glfluee — gleeful

Day 84

```
G M G + + Y + + + + G + + S T
N O R + + L R + + N + + H N E
I U O + + L E + + I + O O + A
L T V + + U V + + V I + + S S
E H E + + F I + + E T + + + P
V F L + + E + + L P L + + + O
I U E + + C C + + E E + + I + O
R L D E + R D C + + + N + + N
H S R + + U N + + + + + G F
S M I S C O N C E P T I O N U
+ + + + C S W I V E L I N G L
+ + + E + E N O V E L T I E S
+ + + R + + R N O I T P E C E R
+ + P Y L L U F E C A E P + + +
+ + + + + + + + + + + + + + +
```

(Over,Down,Direction)
- GROVELED(3,1,S)
- MISCONCEPTION(2,10,E)
- MOUTHFULS(2,1,S)
- NOVELTIES(7,12,E)
- PEACEFULLY(12,14,W)
- PRECONCEPTION(2,14,NE)
- RECEIVING(3,9,NE)
- RECEPTION(15,13,W)
- RESOURCEFULLY(6,13,N)
- REVELING(7,2,SE)
- SHOVELED(14,1,SW)
- SHRIVELING(1,10,N)
- SWIVELING(6,11,E)
- TEASPOONFULS(15,1,S)

Day 86

Fill in the blanks with words from today's spelling list.
1. Lisa **skillfully** helped Julie braid her hair.
2. Jack's new puppy **eagerly** wagged its tail for a treat.
3. His **courageous** action helped stop the car before it hit the crowd.
4. While were on vacation, we took **advantage** of the pool and hot tub at the hotel.
5. The FedEx driver dropped off the **packages** yesterday.
6. My aunt and uncle used an **orphanage** in China to get their new son.
7. The **images** of the earthquake are horrifying.
8. How many **hostages** were taken in the bank robbery?

Day 88

Unscramble these:
1. gatreos — storage
2. naignmag — managing
3. mrlaulyfh — harmfully
4. eocanturmgeen — encouragement
5. ggrabea — garbage
6. gmereayl — meagerly
7. evgnauaaodst — advantageous
8. ieasvlglr — villagers
9. ikcnapgag — packaging
10. nsgguelaa — languages

Day 91

Fill in the blanks with words from today's spelling list:
1. Be sure to read the label on the container carefully for the correct **dosage**.
2. What's the correct **postage** for this package?
3. Last week's storms really **ravaged** our city.
4. I accidentally **smudged** the window.
5. Have you ever made your hair **straighter** by ironing it?
6. Mom **straightened** Dad's tie before they went to their anniversary party.
7. Allison **laughed** so hard she cried when Steve did his comedy routine.
8. We were **priviledged** to have some private time with the senator on his last visit to our district.

Day 92

```
+ S + G + W + + M + D + G + E
+ + A + N + I I + A + N + G G
+ + + C + I D D U + I + E + A
+ + + + R G G G G N + L + B T
+ + + + E I H D E E L + + U T
+ + + T + T L T U O T + + D A
+ + S + E + H E C R + S + G W
+ + + R + G + + G + G + + E +
+ + + S I + + + + + E + + T N
+ + + A P R I V I L E G E I A
+ + R G N I G D U M S + + N U
+ T + + B U D G I N G + + G G
S + + E G A V A R + + + + + H
+ + + + + + + + + + + + + + T
+ + + + + + + + + + + + + + Y
```

(Over,Down,Direction)
- BUDGETING(14,4,S)
- BUDGING(5,12,E)
- COLLEGE(9,7,NE)
- DAUGHTERS(11,1,SW)
- GRUDGING(11,8,NW)
- MIDGETS(9,1,SW)
- NAUGHTY(15,9,S)
- PRIVILEGE(5,10,E)
- RAVAGE(9,13,W)
- SACRILEGE(2,1,SE)
- SMUDGING(11,11,W)
- STRAIGHTENING(1,13,NE)
- WATTAGE(15,7,N)
- WIDGETS(6,1,SE)

Day 93

Fill in the blank with words from today's spelling list.
1. Jack needs to **weigh** 140 pounds to wrestle at the welterweight level.
2. When we took a trip to Maine this winter, we had a **sleigh** ride.
3. My **neighbor**, Mrs. Reed, makes wonderful chocolate chip cookies.
4. The bald **eagle** is a very graceful bird.
5. We met Emily and Scott for **breakfast** yesterday.
6. At its **peak**, the population of our city was 150,000.
7. Her voice was so quiet, we edged closer to the front so that we could hear her **speak**.
8. Those old floorboards in the attic really **creak**!

Day 95

Unscramble these:
1. hdweige — weighed
2. ledhegis — sleighed
3. eednwkae — weakened
4. ksqauey — squeaky
5. naeedsk — sneaked
6. ckraede — creaked
7. eodoibhnhogr — neighborhood
8. kwdeotao — teakwood
9. ekfra — freak
10. ponesk — spoken

Day 99

```
+  +  +  +  R  +  +  +  +  +  +  +  +  +  C
+  O  +  +  +  E  +  +  +  +  +  +  +  +  O
+  +  V  +  +  +  E  +  P  +  +  +  +  +  S  M
+  +  +  E  +  +  +  +  E  +  +  +  +  P  +  P
C  A  T  E  R  W  A  U  L  E  D  O  +  R  U
D  +  +  +  +  H  N  F  +  L  O  +  E  +  L
E  +  +  +  +  +  A  O  +  K  E  W  +  R  S
L  +  +  +  +  U  +  U  I  +  O  D  +  E  I
L  +  +  L  +  +  E  L  L  +  +  P  V
E  +  +  T  +  +  S  +  F  E  L  +  U  E
P  +  E  +  +  T  +  I  +  D  E  +  L  +
M  D  T  N  E  L  L  E  C  X  E  +  B  S  +
O  +  +  +  U  +  +  +  +  +  +  +  E  +
C  +  +  +  A  +  +  +  +  +  +  +  D  R
+  +  +  C  S  H  R  I  E  K  E  D  +  +  +
```

(Over, Down, Direction)
CATERWAULED(1,5,E)
CAULIFLOWER(4,15,NE)
COMPELLED(1,14,N)
COMPULSIVE(15,1,S)
EXCELLENT(11,12,W)
FAULTED(8,6,SW)
OVERHAULED(2,2,SE)
REBELLION(15,14,NW)
REPELLED(5,1,SE)
REPULSED(14,7,S)
SHRIEKED(5,15,E)
SPOOKIEST(14,3,SW)

Day 101

Fill in the blanks with words from today's spelling list.
1. (**Michael**) and his parents stayed at a **motel** when they visited their relatives in San Diego.
2. The **label** on the soup can says that there are 100 grams of sodium in the soup.
3. We will need to **cancel** our dinner plans with (**answers will vary**).
4. I am hoping to study abroad in **Israel** next year.
5. Kristin was an **angel** to pick me up after school.
6. In the winter, I really like sleeping in my **flannel** pajamas.
7. The atomic symbol for **nickel** is Ni.
8. My mother was asked to be a **model** in the Historical Society's fashion show.

Day 103

Unscramble these:
1. iaacclontlen — cancellation
2. elpeadn — paneled
3. eclecdna — canceled
4. vpieulposr — propulsive
5. perpldoel — propelled
6. eedlexlp — expelled
7. ebeladl — labeled
8. doelmde — modeled
9. renelk — kernel
10. noeolcl — colonel

Day 106

Fill in the blanks using words from today's spelling list.
1. How many **barrels** of oil spilled into the Gulf?
2. Emily and Abby played the role of **damsels** in distress terrifically last night.
3. There were only a few **morsels** of food left after the boys ate.
4. The Queen's **jewels** are on display in the Tower of London.
5. Our batting coach usually **counsels** patience when we're in a hitting slump.
6. I'll need some new **pencils** for next fall.
7. Allison made some **stencils** for us to use when we painted the border in her room.
8. There is going to be a meeting of representatives from all of the student **councils** in our state next month.

Day 108

```
M  +  +  +  +  S  +  C  T  R  +  +  +  +  +
+  A  +  L  L  +  +  U  O  O  +  C  +  +  +
G  +  R  I  E  +  N  L  +  L  +  O  J  +  +
+  N  G  V  +  N  I  +  +  E  O  U  E  +  +
+  I  I  +  E  C  R  +  +  S  S  N  W  +  +
V  +  +  L  N  L  +  E  +  N  L  S  E  +  +
+  +  I  U  E  +  O  W  K  U  I  E  L  L  +
+  N  O  +  +  R  E  U  +  O  P  L  R  +  +
G  C  +  +  A  R  +  S  C  U  I  Y  +  +
+  +  +  S  +  +  A  +  L  P  N  +  +  +
+  S  L  E  S  S  A  T  B  +  Y  G  +  +  +
+  +  L  +  C  H  I  S  E  L  I  N  G  +  +
+  S  +  +  +  +  +  +  +  +  +  +  +  +  +
+  +  +  +  S  N  I  A  L  P  A  H  C  +
+  +  +  +  +  +  +  +  +  +  +  +  +  +  +
```

(Over, Down, Direction)
BARRELING(9,11,NW)
CHAPLAINS(14,14,W)
CHISELING(5,12,E)
COLONEL(8,1,SE)
COUNCILOR(2,9,NE)
COUNSELING(12,2,S)
COUNSELOR(10,9,N)
JEWELRY(13,3,S)
KERNEL(9,7,NW)
MARVELOUSLY(1,1,SE)
PUPILS(11,10,N)
TASSELS(8,11,W)
TUNNELING(9,1,SW)
VIGILS(1,6,NE)
WEASELS(8,7,SW)

Day 111

Unscramble these:
1. eoripus — perilous
2. dbeevdile — bedeviled
3. imelpreid — imperiled
4. onilts — tonsil
5. anocvilziiti — civilization
6. lewcdos — scowled
7. augsr — sugar
8. elrueefd — refueled
9. ldedeu — dueled
10. rueltcy — cruelty

Day 114
Fill in the blank with words from today's spelling list.
1. How many **tulip bulbs** did you plant last fall?
2. The expression on her face was completely **unreadable**.
3. If that statue were to break, it would be **irreplaceable**.
4. When we traveled to Haiti after the earthquake, we found some **indescribably** poor living conditions.
5. First year students at the U.S. Military Academy are often called **plebes**.
6. The first movement starts softly and **builds** to a crescendo.
7. It has been so wet, we haven't been able to plant our soybean **fields** yet.
8. A dictator **wields** all the power in a dictatorship.

Day 115
Unscramble these:
1. mabneaglea — manageable
2. beytriiaald — readability
3. aralegbee — agreeable
4. ltiub — built
5. ugitl — guilt
6. iedelwd — wielded
7. erbilud — builder
8. esiddlhe — shielded
9. bibylripato — probability
10. rfletiuoed — outfielder

Day 116

```
+  +  +  +  +  +  +  +  +  +  +  +  S  +  A
O  U  T  F  I  E  L  D  E  R  S  E  G  E  B
+  C  +  +  S  +  +  +  +  +  I  Y  N  L  I
+  +  H  +  +  C  +  +  +  T  A  +  I  B  L
+  +  G  A  G  +  A  +  I  G  +  E  D  A  I
+  +  +  N  N  N  +  L  R  +  +  L  L  E  T
+  +  +  +  I  G  I  E  D  +  +  D  E  G  I
+  +  +  +  +  B  E  D  +  I  +  I  D  +  E
+  +  +  +  A  A  U  A  L  +  N  N  F  +  S
+  +  B  B  +  +  +  C  B  I  +  G  Y  L  +
+  +  O  L  +  +  +  +  +  L  U  +  T  W  +
+  R  Y  G  N  I  D  L  I  G  E  B  L  O  +
P  G  N  I  D  L  F  I  H  S  +  +  I  N  +
+  +  O  U  T  F  I  E  L  D  +  +  U  K  +
+  +  +  +  +  +  +  +  +  +  +  +  G  +  +
```

(Over,Down,Direction)
ABILITIES(15,1,S)   KNOWLEDGEABLE(14,14,N)
AGREEABLY(11,4,SW)   OUTFIELD(3,14,E)
BUILDING(12,12,NW)   OUTFIELDERS(1,2,E)
CHANGEABLE(2,3,SE)   PROBABILITIES(1,13,NE)
CUBING(8,10,NW)   SCALDING(5,3,SE)
FIELDING(13,9,N)   SHIELDING(10,13,W)
GILDING(10,12,W)   YIELDING(12,3,S)
GUILTY(13,15,N)

Day 119
Unscramble these:
1. feureailnsbf — insufferable
2. relsetayap — separately
3. acmrobelpa — comparable
4. aseeodnlircb — considerable
5. rbilacevees — serviceable
6. neferlouneabc — unenforceable
7. tipsibeiclaa — capabilities
8. snilceaebap — inescapable
9. bblaraee — bearable
10. belynasoaunr — unreasonably

Day 121
Fill in the blanks with words from today's spelling list.
1. During World War II, **vegetable** gardens were some times called Victory gardens.
2. The weather in the south in the spring is sometimes very **unpredictable**.
3. If you're traveling to another country, a good guidebook is an **indispensable** travel companion.
4. While he didn't win the race, he did finish in a **respectable** amount of time.
5. Last winter, after the snowstorm, the roads in the mountains were **impassable** for several weeks.
6. Some products, like **disposable** diapers, are not environmentally friendly.
7. Mark's actions toward Josh were **inexcusable**.
8. Even on weekends, my parents were **invariably** up by six am.

Day 126
Fill in the blank with words from today's spelling list.
1. The new coat of paint made our fence look **presentable** again.
2. When the circus acrobat slipped, the audience gasped **audibly**.
3. Jack and Steve went to play **doubles** tennis with Mark and Scott.
4. That new cell phone is **incredibly** easy to use.
5. Our legislature passed a few laws that seem to be **unenforceable** and should be repealed.
6. It's always a good idea to sign your name **legibly**.
7. During the Middle Ages, **nobles** were the ruling class.
8. How many **rubles** is a US dollar worth?

Day 127
Unscramble these:
1. evsei — sieve
2. rcriinilgtobiiy — incorrigibility
3. gatnliby — tangibly
4. lignientlet — intelligent
5. iuealvlnab — invaluable
6. ebalub — bauble
7. iytoilbn — nobility
8. olbfie — foible
9. eduaiecn — audience
10. idanotiu — audition

Day 128

```
A + Y + S + S + + + T + N W + +
U + + T E L + E R + O + E + +
D + + + I + E O L M + + H + +
I + + + T L U G L B + + P + E
T + + + I B I A A + I + E C S
O + + + L P S B + L + O N + I
R + + I + S + I + I E F + E
I + N + B + + A + G G T + + V
U G + N I E C E L I N + I + E
M + + + S + + + L M + A + E +
+ + + + S + + L + + + + T + S
+ + + + O + E + + + + + + N +
+ + + + P T + + + + + + + + I
+ + + + N A L L E G I A N C E
+ + + I E L B A T S N O C + +
```

(Over,Down,Direction)
ALLEGIANCE(6,14,E)
AUDITORIUM(1,1,S)
CONSTABLE(13,15,W)
FOIBLES(13,7,NW)
INTANGIBILITY(15,13,NW)
INTELLIGENCE(4,15,NE)
LEGALITIES(6,2,SE)
NEPHEW(13,6,N)
NIECE(4,9,E)
POSSIBILITIES(5,13,N)
PSALM(6,6,SE)
SALMON(7,6,NE)
SIEVE(15,5,S)
TROUBLING(10,1,SW)

Day 131

Write the words which are combined to make the contraction shown.

1. It's — **It is**
2. They're — **They are**
3. There's — **There is**
4. You're — **You are**
5. We're — **We are**
6. He's — **He is**
7. She's — **She is**
8. Here're — **Here are**

Day 132

```
S E N S I B I L I T I E S + N
I Y + + + + + + + + + + E +
A R S E I C A L L A F + G + E
P A R + V + M P + D + L D V +
P N + E + I S U E + I + I + +
R O + + S A S I S G + S V + +
E I + + L P F N E T N + I + +
H S + M + I O N E E A + D + +
E I + + R + C N H F + C E + +
N V + R + E + E S + E + H + +
S + E H O R R I F I E D + E +
I T + + + P + + S T B E D + +
O + + + M + + + + + + L + + +
N + + O + + + + + + + E + + +
+ + C + + + + + + + + + + + +
```

(Over,Down,Direction)
APPREHENSION(1,3,S)
COMPREHENSIVE(3,15,NE)
DEBTS(13,12,W)
DEFENSIVE(12,11,NW)
DIVIDE(13,4,S)
FALLACIES(11,3,W)
HORRIFIED(4,11,E)
IRRESPONSIBLE(1,2,SE)
MUSTACHE(7,4,SE)
NEGLIGENCE(15,1,SW)
PSALM(8,4,SW)
SENSIBILITIES(1,1,E)
TERRIFIED(2,12,NE)
VISIONARY(2,10,N)

Day 134

Fill in the blanks with words from today's spelling list.
1. How can we **possibly** thank you for all your help?
2. Allison seemed to have an **inexhaustible** supply of energy as we worked refinishing the desk.
3. Emma got her learner's **permit** yesterday.
4. It's very difficult to get along with someone as **inflexible** as she is.
5. Dressed in camouflage, the soldier was almost imperceptible to the enemy.
6. Our attorney said that the evidence would be **inadmissible** in court.
7. Sam drove one of the **convertibles** in the homecoming parade.
8. Jody's pet fawn sometimes **nibbles** the bushes.

Day 135

Unscramble these:

1. obistyspiil — possibility
2. eeduc — deuce
3. monpsrsiei — permission
4. tncpemtebloi — contemptible
5. oscetilbbum — combustible
6. bbeladb — babbled
7. fdeu — feud
8. edlqubib — quibbled
9. ticuniirsylidbett — indestructibility
10. tlpybilaisiu — plausibility

Day 137

Fill in the blank with words from today's spelling list.
1. Aunt Fran made really good peach cobbler for dessert.
2. At the end of the day, I like to sink into a fragrant bubble bath.
3. Jim and Tim can sometimes be **double trouble.** It must be be cause they're twins!
4. Our baseball teams were both idle today.
5. In my horseback riding class, I learned how to saddle and **bridle** my horse today.
6. Uncle Dan really likes to play **golf**. He's a good **golfer**.
7. Jessica likes to **doodle** when she's waiting for the doctor.
8. If we **dawdle** too long, we won't get home in time for supper.

Day 139

Unscramble these:

1. bbuldeb — bubbled
2. cbebhldo — hobbled
3. cnsstoeobleb — cobblestones
4. edelhwed — wheedled
5. lsddie — sidled
6. leogdf — golfed
7. irepldef — pilfered
8. daeddlw — dawdled
9. nodeol — noodle
10. eweelddh — wheedled

Day 140

```
+ + + + + + + + + + + + D G + I
+ + F E U D E D + + + + + A N + D
T R O U B L I N G + + + W I G L
+ + + + + + + + + + + + D L N I
+ + + + + + + + + + + G L D I N
+ + + + S + G + + + N + I E F G
+ + + + + E + O + + + N E L + +
+ + + + + + V R B + + G H O + +
S E N O T S E L B B O C W G E +
+ + + + + F B + O + L + + Z + +
+ G N I L D A R C W + I I + + +
+ + + I + + + + + + I + E L + +
+ + P + + + + + + + D O R + G +
+ + + + + + + + + + D A + E + +
+ + + + + + + + + + I + + L + W +
```

(Over,Down,Direction)
BRIDAL(7,10,SE)
COBBLESTONES(12,9,W)
CRADLING(9,11,W)
DAWDLING(12,1,S)
FEUDED(3,2,E)
GOBBLING(7,6,SE)
GOLFING(14,9,N)
IDLING(15,1,S)
IDOLIZE(9,15,NE)
PILFERING(3,13,NE)
TROUBLING(1,3,E)
WEREWOLVES(14,15,NW)
WHEEDLING(13,9,N)

Day 143
Fill in the blank with words from today's spelling list.
1. Last summer, I worked on an oil rig in the **Gulf of Mexico**.
2. When the firefighters arrived, the whole building was **engulfed** in flames.
3. After the movie, we **indulged** our craving for ice cream.
4. Before winter came, Dad **calked or caulked** all our windows and doors.
5. Paul Bunyan and his Blue Ox are part of Minnesota **folklore**.
6. The **polka** is a German **folk** dance.
7. Jack took the **helm** of the sailboat so Dave could trim the sails.
8. My aunt was overwhelmed at the outpouring of support for my uncle after his accident.

Day 145
Fill in the blank using words from today's spelling list.
1. One of the first things I learned in first aid was how to take my **pulse**.
2. Last night, I had a sudden **impulse** to go for a bike ride.
3. Do you like sweet or **salty** snacks better? I like the **salt** in pretzels.
4. Steve and Jon played sentries in the school play. They had one line, "**Halt**! Who goes there?"
5. The traffic tie up wasn't our **fault**, but it still made us late for the train.
6. The jury convicted him of **assault** on a policeman and sentenced him to three months in jail.
7. Have you ever visited **Sault Ste. Marie**, Michigan?
8. Let's hope that the snow **melt** won't cause too much flooding this spring.

Day 147
Unscramble these:
1. corih — choir
2. pielumvis — impulsive
3. sneuvdloc — convulsed
4. ddefaeult — defaulted
5. srdoaeseultm — somersaulted
6. treselsw — swelters
7. eteldp — pelted
8. terlhse — shelter
9. dxleeat — exalted
10. mdeelt — melted

Day 149
Fill in the blanks with words from today's spelling list.
1. Sarah's announcement came like a **bolt** out of the blue.
2. A bird will **molt** at least once a year.
3. Allison will need to wait until next week for the **result** of her blood test.
4. Sometimes, it's **difficult** to overlook an **insult** like that.
5. I hope that we can **solve** this problem ourselves with out involving an **adult**.
6. We need to stop at the drugstore and get some **salve** for your sunburn.

Day 151
Unscramble these:
1. iitlfceusfdi — difficulties
2. dewaltz — waltzed
3. elvacs — calves
4. ueotdcnls — consulted
5. itrlovenou — revolution
6. emdtol — molted
7. sluteedr — resulted
8. aaletcdutp — catapulted
9. ccotul — occult
10. basevlod — absolved

Day 152

```
+ + + + + + + + + + + + R N S
+ + G + + + + + + + + + E S O
+ + N + + + + + W + V + + E I L
+ + + I + R A + O + + + V T U
+ + + + T L E L + G + L U I
N O I T A T L U S N O C A L I
+ + + + Z S T U I U + + H O O
+ + + I R I T P + L + + S N +
+ + N I O + L + G A + T + B +
+ G O N + U + + N T + + I A +
+ H A + S + + + + I A + N +
C R G N I T L O M + + T C + G
Y + I S P A G H E T T I L + +
+ + + + + + + + + + + + + O +
+ + + + + + + + + + + + + J
```

(Over,Down,Direction)
ABSOLUTION(14,10,N)
CATAPULTING(13,12,NW)
CHOIRS(1,12,NE)
CONSULTATION(12,6,W)
HALVES(13,7,N)
INSULTING(3,13,NE)
JOLTING(15,15,NW)
MOLTING(9,12,W)
RESULTING(7,4,SE)
REVOLUTIONARY(13,1,SW)
SOLUTION(15,1,S)
SPAGHETTI(4,13,E)
WALTZING(9,3,SW)

Day 154

List the contraction that is formed by the two words

1. They are — **They're**
2. There is — **There's**
3. There are — **There're**
4. It is — **It's**
5. Is not — **Isn't**
6. You are — **You're**
7. We are — **We're**
8. Were not — **Weren't**

Day 156

```
I W + + + + + + + + S G + N E
T S I + + + + + + + Y N O + X
E R + G + + + G + S I N + C
M E + + W + + N + + T M O + L
I M + + + A I + + A E M I + A
Z I + + + M M + M + M A T + M
A A + + I + + A + + A R A + A
T L + A + + L + + + T G M + T
I C M + + C + + + + I O A + I
O S + + E + + + + + C R L + O
N I + R B A L S A M A P C + N
+ D L A C I T A M E L B O R P
+ + + + + + + + + + L + R + +
+ + + + + + + + + + Y + P + +
+ + + A C C L A M A T I O N +
```

(Over,Down,Direction)
ACCLAMATION(4,15,E)   MAIMING(3,9,NE)
BALSAM(5,11,E)   PROBLEMATICAL(15,12,W)
DISCLAIMERS(2,12,N)   PROCLAMATION(13,14,N)
EXCLAMATION(15,1,S)   PROGRAMMING(12,11,N)
ITEMIZATION(1,1,S)   RECLAMATION(4,11,NE)
                         SYSTEMATICALLY(11,1,S)
                         WIGWAM(2,1,SE)

Day 157

Choose the correct pronoun in the sentences below:

1. I have a strong dislike for people **who** lie to me.
2. Many of you have a friend with **whom** you trust your deepest secrets.
3. Just looking at an airplane scares someone **who** is afraid of flying.
4. **Whom** did you say was calling?
5. The thief, **who** stole the bicycle, was caught.
6. To **whom** should I give this letter?
7. I know the actor **who** has the lead in that movie.
8. My grandmother, **whom** I loved very much, died last summer.

Day 159

Unscramble these:

1. ntmiaae — animate
2. oraiyfmlnl — informally
3. tsrthrommeee — thermometers
4. maapsibtl — baptismal
5. ioxaitacm — axiomatic
6. isdoim — idioms
7. rmupemi — premium
8. ruianmu — uranium
9. gmauiern — geranium
10. emordasn — ransomed

Day 162

Fill in the blank with words from today's spelling list:

1. We are going to visit the **planetarium** the next time we're in the city.
2. Last winter, my parents went to Belgium to attend a health care **symposium**.
3. How much do you think Tim **remembers** of his accident?
4. This year, we are growing green beans, peas, **cucumbers**, and tomatoes in our garden.
5. After we **assembled** the bunk bed, we had to **disassemble** it.
6. Our lake house has exposed **timbers** in the living room.
7. **Gamblers** will like the new casino that they're building in the city.
8. **Ambergris** is an ingredient in perfume that prevents evaporation.

Day 163

```
M + + + + + + + + + + + D S
U + + + + + + + + + + E + E
I + + + + + + + + + L + S P
R E M E M B E R E D B + C + T
O + N + M + + + + M + R + R E
P A + C + U + + E + A + E C M
M + S + U + I S + M + B + H B
E + + S + M S R B + M + A E
+ + + + E A B L A E + + M R
+ + + + S M E E V U + + B +
+ + + I D B O R + Q + + E +
+ D + + + N L + E + A + R +
M U I R A L O S Y + D + + +
L U M B E R E D + + + + + +
+ + + + + + + + + + + + + +
```

(Over,Down,Direction)
AQUARIUM(12,12,NW)   ENCUMBERED(2,4,SE)
ASSEMBLY(2,6,SE)   LUMBERED(1,14,E)
CHAMBER(14,6,S)   NOVEMBER(7,12,NE)
DISASSEMBLED(3,12,NE)   REMEMBERED(1,4,E)
EMPORIUM(1,8,N)   SCRAMBLED(14,3,SW)
                         SEPTEMBER(15,1,S)
                         SOLARIUM(8,13,W)

Day 165

Fill in the blank with words from today's spelling list.

1. My grandmother thinks I **resemble** my mom more than my dad.
2. Most of these clothes can be **tumble** dried.
3. When we were hiking, the large tree root caused me to **stumble** and fall.
4. What's the **theme** of the graduation party?
5. Appendicitis can sometimes cause **extreme** stomach pain.
6. Do you have a favorite **perfume**? Mine is Chanel No. 5.
7. One of my little brother's chores is to **empty** the trash each week.
8. After listening to the crowd **grumble** about the delay, the band decided to resume playing.

Day 167

Unscramble these:

1. urpseem — supreme
2. dlebhum — humbled
3. ustledmb — stumbled
4. legmirbsne — resembling
5. iosmpatnsu — assumption
6. txetrymie — extremity
7. rdsemuep — presumed
8. npsoimtnocu — consumption
9. ohgtte — ghetto
10. ptemeid — emptied

Day 168

```
E + + + C O S T U M I N G G +
+ C + + + + + + Y + + O N N +
+ + N + + + + L + + + I + I +
+ + + A + + E + + + L T + M +
S + + + L M + + B + P + U + +
+ P + + E B + + M + + M S + +
+ + A R + + M U + + + U T S +
+ + P G + G R E H + + S U A +
+ U + + H + N U S + + E M + +
S + + + + E M I + E R B + + +
+ + + + B T + L + R P L + + +
+ + + + L + + T + B + I + + +
+ + + I + + + + I + M + N + +
+ G N I Y T P M E + + U G + +
+ G + N I M B L Y + + + M + +
```

(Over,Down,Direction)
ASSUMING(14,8,N)
COSTUMING(5,1,E)
EMPTYING(9,14,W)
HUMBLING(9,8,SW)
MUMBLING(13,15,NW)
NIMBLY(4,15,E)
PRESUMPTION(12,11,N)
RESEMBLANCE(11,11,NW)
RUMBLING(7,8,NE)
SPAGHETTI(1,5,SE)
STUMBLING(13,6,S)
SUPREMELY(1,10,NE)

Day 170

Unscramble these:
1. emrpspa — pampers
2. riheswmp — whimpers
3. ormpser — rompers
4. smeisrp — simpers
5. alypm — amply
6. smeapls — samples
7. snouaitmn — mountains
8. rcaynltie — certainly
9. antufions — fountains
10. bgsaainr — bargains

Day 174

Fill in the blank using words from today's spelling list.
1. The **Republicans** and the Democrats are the two major political parties in the United States.
2. We enjoy drinking **Colombia** coffee.
3. Residents of Canada are called **Canadians**.
4. Since her family is from Norway, my mom sometimes wears a traditional **Norwegian** costume.
5. Genghis Khan was from **Mongolia**.
6. When we went to beach last summer, we saw lots of **pelican** near the pier.
7. I helped my mom sew new **curtains** for the kitchen.
8. My sister Katie met lots of **Australians** when she visited Australia last year.

Day 175

Unscramble these:
1. tanBrii — Britain
2. atcedinpa — captained
3. franfiu — ruffian
4. ygooleth — theology
5. eirbtrnnua — interurban
6. abairAn — Arabian
7. sCiraithn — Christian
8. noogaMlin — Mongolian
9. elegclo — college
10. iandanl — Indiana

Day 177

Fill in the blank with words from today's spelling list.
1. When did **electric** lights come to your dad's farm?
2. Do you like classical **music**? I do.
3. **Asia** is the largest of the seven continents.
4. The economy was the most important **issue** in the campaign last fall.
5. Janet carefully unwrapped the **tissue** from her gift.
6. **Frijoles** is the Spanish word for beans.
7. Sometimes I think I need a **magic** wand to get all my projects done.
8. Jack's favorite subject is **arithmetic**.

Day 178

Unscramble these:
1. oiitpilanc — politician
2. cumaiisn — musician
3. osiirtneactb — obstetrician
4. acnyishpi — physician
5. gicaainm — magician
6. cetilceianr — electrician
7. sinarEua — Eurasian
8. iPninaheoc — Phoenician
9. rnPsiae — Persian
10. iucCasana — Caucasian

Day 179

```
S + + O M A G I C I A N S P D
N + + B + + + + + + + T + A E
A + + S + + N + + + A + + R U
I + + T + + + O + T + + + I S
C + + E O + + + I + + + + S S
I + + T + P + S + H + + S I I
T + + R + + T + + + S N + A +
I + + I + I + I + + A U + N +
L + + C C + + + C I + + C S +
O + + I S N A I C I N H C E T
P + A A + + + U + A + + + + +
+ N + N + + F + + + + N + + +
S + + S + N D E N O I H S A F
+ + + + O + + + + + + + + + +
+ + + C + + + + + + + + + + +
```

(Over,Down,Direction)
CONFUCIANS(4,15,NE)
CUSHION(13,9,NW)
FASHIONED(15,13,W)
ISSUED(15,6,N)
MAGICIANS(5,1,E)
OBSTETRICIANS(4,1,S)
OPTICIANS(5,5,SE)
PARISIANS(14,1,S)
POLITICIANS(1,11,N)
STATISTICIANS(13,1,SW)
TECHNICIANS(15,10,W)

Frequently Used Spelling Rules

FLOSS RULE
A one-syllable base word with one short vowel immediately before the final sounds of (f), (l), or (s) is spelled with ff, ll, or ss.
Examples:
off
ball
miss
Exceptions to this rule: yes, gas, bus, plus, this

RABBIT RULE
Double the consonants b, d, g, m, n and p after a short vowel in a two syllable word.
Examples:
rabbit
manner
dagger
banner
drummer

DOUBLING RULE
A base word ending in one consonant after an accented short vowel doubles the final consonant before a suffix beginning with a vowel.
Examples:
run + ing = running
stop + ed = stopped
hop + ing = hopping

DROPPING RULE
A base word ending in silent "e" drops "e" before a suffix beginning with a vowel.
Examples.
hope + ing = hoping
shine + ing = shining
slope + ed = sloped

CHANGING RULE
A base word ending in "y" after a consonant changes "y" to "i" before any suffix (except one beginning with "i").
Examples:
baby + ies = babies
lady + ies = ladies
boy + s = boys
toy + s = toys

Remember: You change the babies not the boys!